OECD Health Policy Studies

The Looming Crisis In the Health Workforce

HOW CAN OECD COUNTRIES RESPOND?

ORGANISATION FOR ECONOMIC CO-OPERATION AND DEVELOPMENT

The OECD is a unique forum where the governments of 30 democracies work together to address the economic, social and environmental challenges of globalisation. The OECD is also at the forefront of efforts to understand and to help governments respond to new developments and concerns, such as corporate governance, the information economy and the challenges of an ageing population. The Organisation provides a setting where governments can compare policy experiences, seek answers to common problems, identify good practice and work to co-ordinate domestic and international policies.

The OECD member countries are: Australia, Austria, Belgium, Canada, the Czech Republic, Denmark, Finland, France, Germany, Greece, Hungary, Iceland, Ireland, Italy, Japan, Korea, Luxembourg, Mexico, the Netherlands, New Zealand, Norway, Poland, Portugal, the Slovak Republic, Spain, Sweden, Switzerland, Turkey, the United Kingdom and the United States. The Commission of the European Communities takes part in the work of the OECD.

OECD Publishing disseminates widely the results of the Organisation's statistics gathering and research on economic, social and environmental issues, as well as the conventions, guidelines and standards agreed by its members.

This work is published on the responsibility of the Secretary-General of the OECD. The opinions expressed and arguments employed herein do not necessarily reflect the official views of the Organisation or of the governments of its member countries.

Also available in French under the title:

Études de l'OCDE sur les politiques de santé

Les personnels de santé dans les pays de l'OCDE

COMMENT RÉPONDRE À LA CRISE IMMINENTE ?

Foreword

This publication examines the relationship between the international migration of health workers – both within the OECD area and between the rest of the world and the OECD area – and health workforce policies in OECD countries. It assesses how the supply of health workers, particularly that of doctors and nurses, has adjusted to demand in different countries, taking account of migration among other inflows and outflows of health professionals.

The report is one of the main outputs of a project on health workforce policies and international migration, which was undertaken by the OECD in co-operation with the WHO between 2005 and 2008. This publication draws from and is the synthesis of various OECD analyses. First, it uses the findings of a chapter in the 2007 Edition of the International Migration Outlook on "Immigrant Health Workers in OECD Countries in the Broader Context of Highly-skilled Migration", which had reviewed recent migration flows and policies for health workers in OECD countries, based on data on the stock of doctors and nurses by country of training/birth. Second, the report builds from case studies on workforce policies and international migration in Canada, France, Italy, New Zealand, the United Kingdom, the United States. Third, it reviews previous OECD analysis on the supply of physician services in OECD countries, ways to tackle nurse shortages, and the health workforce skill mix, as well as relevant policy studies and academic literature.

Within the OECD, the work has been undertaken jointly by the Health Division and by the International Migration and Non-member Economies Division, of the Directorate for Employment, Labour and Social Affairs. The main authors of the report are, in alphabetical order, Francesca Colombo, Jean-Christophe Dumont, Jeremy Hurst and Pascal Zurn. Christine Le Thi provided statistical assistance, and Gabrielle Luthy provided secretarial support. The team is grateful for the support and advice received from Elizabeth Docteur, Martine Durand, Jean-Pierre Garson, John Martin and Peter Scherer.

Acknowledgements

The OECD *project on International Migration and Health Workforce Policies has been funded partly by regular contributions from member countries of the OECD. Additional voluntary contributions to the project were made by the following member countries: Australia, Canada, New Zealand and Switzerland.*

The project was undertaken jointly by the OECD and the World Health Organization: one of the authors of this report, Pascal Zurn, is a WHO official who was seconded to the OECD to work on the project. We are grateful to the Swiss authorities for the financial contribution which supported this secondment.

The project has also been co-financed by a grant provided by the Directorate General for Health and Consumer Protection of the European Commission. Nonetheless, the views expressed in this report should not be taken to reflect the official position of the European Union.

Table of Contents

Boxes

Table

Figures

This book has...

StatLinks

A service that delivers Excel® files
from the printed page!

Look for the *StatLinks* at the bottom right-hand corner of the tables or graphs in this book.
To download the matching Excel® spreadsheet, just type the link into your Internet browser,
starting with the ***http://dx.doi.org*** prefix.
If you're reading the PDF e-book edition, and your PC is connected to the Internet, simply
click on the link. You'll find *StatLinks* appearing in more OECD books.

ISBN 978-92-64-05043-3
The Looming Crisis in the Health Workforce:
How Can OECD Countries Respond?
© OECD 2008

Introduction and Main Findings

Introduction

OECD countries face a challenge in responding to the demand for health workers over the next 20 years. This challenge arises in a world which is already characterised by significant international migration of health workers, both across OECD countries and between some developing countries and the OECD area. Whether these migration flows increase or decrease over the next 20 years is likely to depend largely on what combination of human-resource management policies and migration policies is adopted by OECD countries.

Raising domestic training rates in OECD countries could contribute to filling the gap and would reduce the "pull factors" on migration. But, the duration of medical training will limit the potential impact of increasing training in the short run. Migration may continue to play a role, at least in some OECD countries, in managing temporary disequilibria or addressing regional imbalances. However, other domestic human resource policies can also contribute to meeting the increasing demand for health workers. Improving retention, adapting skill mix or making better use of people with foreign qualifications could, to some extent, help to match the supply to the demand for health workers. In this context, good practices need to be identified and their transferability evaluated.

In any case, the management of health human resources cannot be considered in isolation, due to the increasing interdependency between countries through international migration of highly-skilled workers in general, and health professionals in particular. Equity concerns with regard to lower income countries, some of which face severe shortages of doctors and nurses, are growing too. This suggests a strong case for better international co-operation.

Push factors in origin countries also contribute to generating high levels of migration. However, health workforce policies in origin countries are not the focus of this report. This is not to say that this report is oblivious of these complex and serious issues. In fact, to the extent that they shape the international debate on the management of health workforce, these "push factors" have informed the discussion of policies in this report.

This report analyses international migration and training of health workers in the context of other workforce policies, focusing on doctors and nurses.* It starts in Chapter 1 with a review of the recent and expected evolution in the density of doctors and nurses. Chapter 2 analyses education and migration policies and their interactions, in light of past

---

* Migration flows and workforce management also concern other important health professional categories, such as pharmacists, dentists, physiotherapists, as well as caregivers taking care of the dependent elderly. This report focuses on doctors and nurses, for which data have been collected and can be shown to support the analysis. Some data on foreign-born pharmacists and dentists collected for the year 2000 are however reported in other OECD work (Dumont and Zurn, 2007).

trends. Chapter 3 reviews other health workforce policies aiming at an efficient use of the available health resources. Challenges related to international equity and interdependency dimensions are discussed in Chapter 4. The last chapter concludes by offering options for addressing future health workforce needs.

Main findings

- The average growth in physician and nurse density in the OECD area slowed sharply in the past 15 years compared with the previous 15 years. The trends for physicians were accompanied by changes in lifetime hours worked, growing feminisation of the workforce, increasing specialisation, and a growing number of health workers' retirements.

- Circa 2000, several OECD countries reported shortages of doctors and nurses and published projections suggesting future shortages of health workers.

- UN population projections suggest that younger age cohorts will shrink in many OECD countries over the next 20 years, possibly increasing cross-sector competition to recruit the best and the brightest students.

- Despite differences in how medical and nursing education is organised, most OECD countries exercise some form of control over student intakes, either by capping the total number of places or by limiting financial support to medical education. Intake to medical schools has followed a U-shape curve in many OECD countries, with a downswing in the 1980s and early 1990s and an upswing around the end of the last decade. Because of the long delay in training, the upswing has only recently become identifiable in graduation rates in a few countries. In fact, on average across the OECD, the number of medical graduates in 2005 lies below the 1985 level.

- Despite recent upward trends in doctors' and nurses' training rates, potential gaps between the demand for, and the supply of, health professionals may emerge in the future in light of demographic changes and increasing income. This calls for a continuous policy emphasis on maintaining training capacity for both doctors and nurses.

- The contribution of foreign-trained doctors to changes in stocks of physicians is significant and has increased over time in many OECD countries. In several OECD countries, immigration jumped sharply at about the time that shortages were identified at the end of the 1990s. Continuing or even greater reliance on migration of health professionals could make health systems in certain OECD countries too dependent on immigration.

- Migration and training policies should not be considered as the only possible solutions. Other policies aiming at a better use of the available health workforce are also called for. These include: i) improving retention (particularly through better workforce organisation and management policies, in particular in remote and rural areas); ii) enhancing integration in the health workforce (e.g., by attracting back those who have left the health workforce and by improving the procedures for recognising and as necessary supplementing foreign qualifications of immigrant health professionals); iii) adopting a more efficient skill mix (e.g., by developing the role of advanced practice nurses and physicians' assistants); and iv) improving productivity (e.g., through linking payment to performance). Different countries are likely to choose different mixes of these policies, depending, among other things, on the flexibility of their health labour markets, institutional constraints, and cost.

- Increasing international mobility and the emergence of shortages of health professionals in many OECD countries and worldwide have raised concerns about international interdependency in the management of health human resources. There is indeed a risk for shortages to be exported within and beyond the OECD area, putting excessive burden on the poorest countries in the world. This risk exists also in the case where OECD countries attract health workers mainly from a limited number of large-supply origin countries which offer training programmes aimed at "exporting" health professionals.

- Even if the global health workforce shortage goes far beyond the migration issue, international migration can contribute to exacerbating the severity of the problems in some countries with low starting densities of health professionals. This raises equity concerns. However, strategies and practices implemented at both national and international level, such as codes of conduct, raise unresolved conceptual and practical implementation challenges. International development initiatives can help to strengthen health systems in origin countries, thereby mitigating factors which are pushing health professionals to leave.

- Possible solutions to address structural imbalances between the supply of and the demand for health professionals do not carry equal weight, since implementing them involves trade-offs between different policy objectives, both at domestic and international levels.

- A strong case can therefore be made for better international monitoring and communication about health workforce policy and movements of health professionals across countries, with a view to diagnosing potential imbalances between demand and supply in the global market for health workers and improving the prospects for international co-ordination.

ISBN 978-92-64-05043-3
The Looming Crisis in the Health Workforce:
How Can OECD Countries Respond?
© OECD 2008

Chapter 1

Health Workforce Demographics: An Overview

This chapter presents data on the health workforces in OECD countries, including cross-country variation, past trends, and projections over the next 20 years. On average, there has been a prolonged growth in physician and nurse density in OECD countries over the past 30 years but the growth rates have slowed sharply since the early 1990s. Cost containment policies, such as control of entry into medical school in the case of doctors, and closure of hospital beds in the case of nurses, may explain much of the slowdown. By 2000, several OECD countries were reporting shortages of doctors and nurses and some countries published projections of the supply and demand for doctors suggesting that as a result of the anticipated retirement of health workers and increasing demand for their services, shortages would increase unless training rates were raised. Meanwhile, UN population projections suggest that between 2005 and 2025, younger age cohorts in the population will shrink in many OECD countries.

1. Cross-country variations and evolution of physician and nurse densities

There is a wide variation in the reported density of both doctors and nurses across OECD countries. Figure 1.1 shows that in the case of doctors, the range in the ratio of practicing physicians per 1 000 population was over threefold, from 1.5 in Turkey to 4.9 in Greece in 2005. The average density of the OECD area was 3.0. Figure 1.2 shows that in the case of nurses, the reported range in density was more than eightfold, from 1.8 practicing nurses per 1 000 population in Turkey to 15.4 in Norway in 2005. The average density over the OECD area was 8.9.[1]

Figure 1.3 shows that in the past 3 decades, there has been a prolonged increase in physician density in all OECD countries for which data are available. In most OECD countries, physician density grew more quickly in the 15 years from 1975 to 1990, at an

Figure 1.1. **Practicing physicians per 1 000 population, 2005
or latest year available**

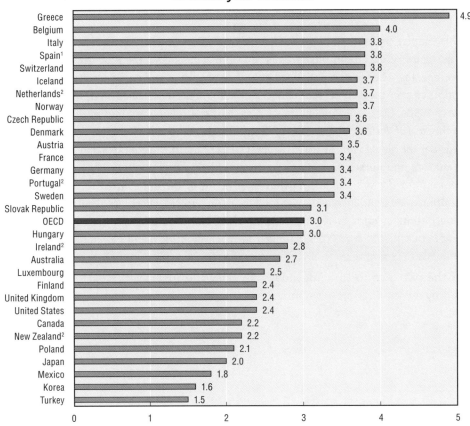

StatLink http://dx.doi.org/10.1787/447675150143

1. Data for Spain include dentists and stomatologists.
2. Ireland, the Netherlands, New Zealand and Portugal provide the number of all physicians entitled to practice rather than only those practicing.

Source: OECD (2007b), *Health at a Glance*, Paris.

Figure 1.2. **Practicing nurses per 1 000 population, 2005 or latest year available**

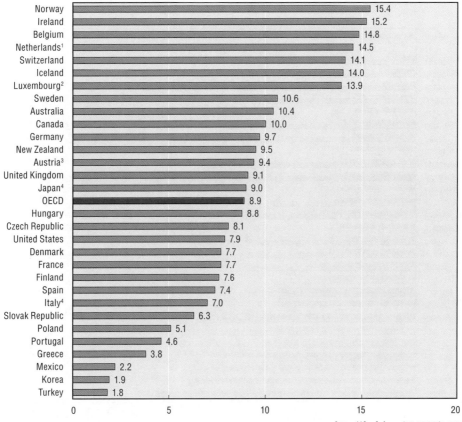

StatLink http://dx.doi.org/10.1787/447727564828

1. The Netherlands reports all nurses entitled to practice rather than those practicing only.
2. Luxembourg includes nursing aids.
3. Austria reports only nurses employed in hospitals.
4. The calculation of average annual growth rate for Japan and Italy is based on a slightly different time period to avoid a break in series resulting from methodological changes.

Source: OECD (2007b), Health at a Glance, Paris.

average rate just over 3.0% per annum, than in the 15 years from 1990 to 2005, when the average was 1.6% per annum. Figure 1.4 shows that in the case of nurses, average density also grew more quickly, on average, in the earlier period (1975-1990), at 2.6% per annum, than in the later period (1990-2005) when it grew at 1.6% per annum.

Over the past two to three decades, the growth in physician headcounts has been influenced by a combination of factors including demand changes (themselves driven by factors such as rising incomes, changing medical technology, ageing of the population) and supply factors (such as controls on entry to medical schools,[2] immigration and emigration and changes in physician productivity).

In general, the average growth in physician density has been slower than the average growth in real health expenditure per capita in the OECD area but faster than the likely effect of the ageing of the population on health expenditure,[3] except in some countries where significant ageing is occurring in the patient population (Figure 1.5).

Changes in hours worked per physician may have played a role in raising the demand for doctors in terms of headcount. Anecdotally, young physicians today are often said to wish to work shorter hours than their predecessors did, even if little evidence for changes

Figure 1.3. **Change in practicing physician density, 1975-1990 and 1990-2005**

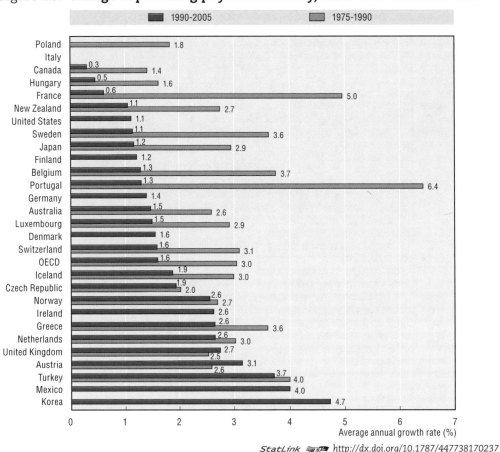

StatLink 〰️ http://dx.doi.org/10.1787/447738170237

Note: Ireland, the Netherlands, New Zealand and Portugal provide the number of all physicians entitled to practice rather than only those practicing.
The OECD consistent average is calculated for 20 countries.
Source: OECD Health Data 2007.

in average working hours per physician was found in a selection of European countries between 1992 and 2000, using the Eurostat Labour Force Survey (OECD, 2006a). Legislative changes with respect to working hours for junior doctors or other health professionals in general have occurred in the EU context with the Working Time Directive[4] and also in the United States.[5] On the other hand, in Australia average weekly working hours for clinicians fell from 48 in 1997 to 44.6 in 2003, a decline of about 7% (Lennon, 2005). And in Canada, a study for the city of Winnipeg suggested that family physicians in the age group 30-49 years provided 20% less patient visits per year than their same-age peers did ten years previously (although older physicians provided 33% more visits than their same-age peers a decade earlier) (Watson *et al.*, 2004).

Growing feminisation of the physician workforce and growing part-time working is also likely to have reduced lifetime hours worked. On average, female physicians work fewer weekly hours than male physicians in many OECD countries (OECD, 2006a). Also, on average, female physicians have shorter working lives than male physicians. Figure 1.6 shows changes in the female proportion of the physician workforce in OECD countries in 1990 and 2005. On average, the proportion of females in the physician workforce increased by around 30% – from 28.7% to 38.3% over this period.

Figure 1.4. **Change in nurses density, 1975-1990 and 1990-2005**

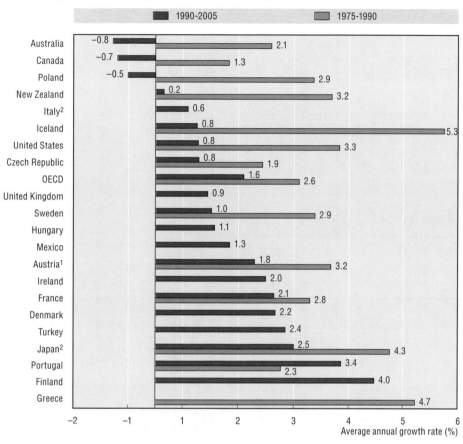

Note: OECD consistent average is calculated for 12 countries.
1. Austria reports only nurses employed in hospitals.
2. The calculation of average annual growth rate for Japan and Italy is based on a slightly different time period to avoid a break in series resulting from methodological changes.
Source: OECD Health Data 2007.

The health workforce in OECD countries is ageing as the "baby boom" generation of health workers begins to reach retirement age. Figures A1a-b in Annex A show for a selection of OECD countries how the age- distributions of health workers have (in most cases) been shifting to the right in the last decade, or so. This means not only that the average age of health workers has been increasing, but also that a growing proportion of health workers are now in their 50s or early 60s and may be expected to retire in the next decade or so.

Increasing specialisation in the medical profession may also have raised the demand for doctors. The ratio of specialists to general practitioners rose from 1.5 to 2.0 between 1990 and 2005 on average among OECD countries. Growing specialisation, which goes hand in hand with expanding technology, encourages additional activity and referrals and may require doctors in large numbers where 24-hour cover of the full range of acute specialties is required in hospitals.

In the case of nurses, the growth (or shrinkage) in headcounts in the period 1990-2005 can be explained by the same factors as for doctors. However, rising demand may have been offset to a greater extent than in the case of doctors by productivity

Figure 1.5. **Real GDP per capita and practicing physicians density, 1975 to 2005 in selected OECD countries**

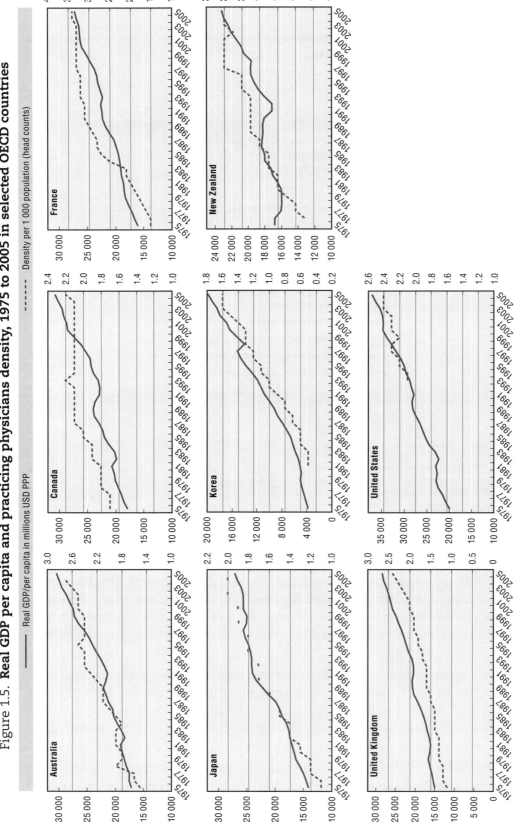

Source: OECD Health Data 2007.

StatLink http://dx.doi.org/10.1787/448018720576

Figure 1.6. **Women physicians as a percentage of total physicians, OECD countries, 1990 and 2004**

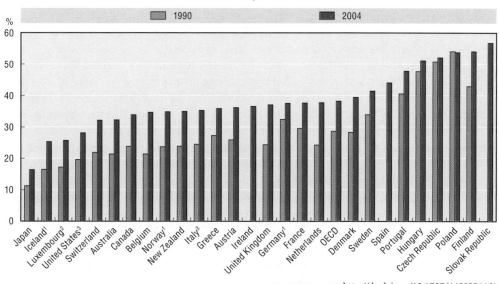

StatLink ⟨⟩ http://dx.doi.org/10.1787/448055446131

1. Data refer to 1991.
2. Data refer to 1992.
3. Data refer to 1993.
Source: OECD Health Data 2007.

improvements. Hospital beds, and some of their accompanying nurses, have been reduced in many OECD countries because of increasing day-case treatment, declining length of stay and the discharge of long-stay patients to residential homes and domiciliary settings.[6]

2. Projections of the demand for supply of doctors and nurses

In many OECD countries the younger age cohorts in the population are expected to decline over the next 20 years (Box 1.1). This increases competition for the best students and may potentially make it more difficult to train and recruit health workers at home. However, in most OECD countries the ratio of medical school places to number of applicants is still pretty low – and this ratio may therefore well increase without any major consequence for medical school intakes. The situation may be different for nurses.

Forecasting future shortages is a challenging task, especially because of difficulties to incorporate changes in productivity. Nevertheless, it is likely that future demand for more and better health care will keep the need for additional physicians at the limits that the economy can sustain (Cooper, 2008).

A number of countries have published projections of demand and/or supply for health professionals. The results of some of these projections are reported below.

In France, the Ministries of Employment, Labour and Social Cohesion and of Health and Social Protection have published projections of *supply* from 2002 to 2025 which suggest that the number of doctors could decline by 9.4% (and medical density by 16%) if the *numerus clausus* were to remain at 7 000 places from 2006 onwards and would still decline by 4.9% (and medical density by 11%) if the *numerus clausus* were increased to 8 000 places – as is currently the Ministry's objective for 2012. This projected decline is partly due to the fact that entry into the second year of medical school has been controlled tightly over the previous two and a half decades. The *numerus clausus* was reduced steadily from around

---

Box 1.1. **Decreasing pool of young cohorts**

UN population projections (using a medium fertility assumption) suggest that in Europe population numbers in the age group 15-24 will decline by about 25% between 2005 and 2025. In Japan numbers in this population group will decline by about 20% and in Korea by 33% over the same period. However, in Australia, Mexico and New Zealand numbers will remain almost constant and in the United States, these are expected to increase by over 8%. The table below shows the relevant UN projections for the population aged 15-24 in all 30 OECD countries. Where the 15-24 age group falls, a rising proportion of young people will have to enter the health profession if current training rates are to be maintained. This will increase competition for the best students, especially when training rates have been raised in order to increase the supply of health professionals, as is the case in several countries. While it is unlikely that there would be a problem in finding applicants to medical school, there could be difficulties in the case of nurses. Some concerns have also been expressed about maintaining the quality of applicants to medical training.

UN projections of population aged 15-24, 2005-2025, OECD countries

	2005	2025	% change 2005-2025		2005	2025	% change 2005-2025
	Population 15-24 (thousands)				Population 15-24 (thousands)		
Australia	2 809	2 874	2.3	Luxembourg	53	66	24.5
Austria	1 001	857	−14.4	Mexico	19 005	19 026	0.1
Belgium	1 255	1 174	−6.5	Netherlands	1 949	1 978	1.5
Canada	4 340	4 104	−5.4	New Zealand	587	602	2.6
Czech Republic	1 350	964	−28.6	Norway	571	611	7.0
Denmark	597	660	10.6	**OECD**	**5 398**	**5 081**	**−8.1**
European OECD countries	**2 816**	**2 442**	**−9.8**	Poland	6 220	3 508	−43.6
Finland	653	599	−8.3	Portugal	1 327	1 138	−14.2
France	7 789	7 909	1.5	Republic of Korea	6 953	4 654	−33.1
Germany	9 761	7 578	−22.4	Slovakia	850	528	−37.9
Greece	1 355	1 089	−19.6	Spain	5 263	4 859	−7.7
Hungary	1 289	957	−25.8	Sweden	1 115	1 093	−2.0
Iceland	43	42	−2.3	Switzerland	892	840	−5.8
Ireland	641	690	7.6	Turkey	13 604	13 280	−2.4
Italy	5 959	5 699	−4.4	United Kingdom	7 841	7 457	−4.9
Japan	14 111	11 124	−21.2	United States	42 759	46 457	8.6

StatLink 🔗 http://dx.doi.org/10.1787/448137544258

Note: Data refers to medium fertility variant.
Source: The 2006 revision population database, United Nations Population division.

---

8 700 in the mid 1970s to around 3 500 in the early 1990s and was held at that level for most of the rest of the 1990s (Cash and Ulmann, 2008).

In Japan, a Special Committee on the Demand and Supply of Doctors set up by the Ministry of Health Labour, and Welfare, has released estimates which suggest that the *supply* of doctors will increase by 21% between 2004 and 2025. The Committee has stated that it expects supply and *demand* to be in balance in 2022.

In the United Kingdom, the "Wanless" report (2002) which set out alternative scenarios for the expansion of the National Health Service suggested that the United Kingdom was short of doctors and nurses. The *demand* for doctors could increase by about 50% between 2005 and 2020. *Supply* might increase by about 27% leading to a projected shortage of doctors of about 20% in 2020 (Wanless, 2002). These projections however may be challenged by more recent trends.

In Canada, the Expert Panel on Health Professional Human Resources was asked to develop medium and long-term strategies to ensure Ontario has sufficient physician resources to meet future health needs. Their findings indicated that Ontario will have by 2010 a shortage ranging from 1 367 to 3 356 physicians, that is between 6% and 15% of the total physicians in Ontario in 2010 (Expert Panel on Health Professional Human Resources, 2001).

In the United States, the Health Resources and Services Administration (HSRA) has estimated that the *demand* for physicians could increase by 22% between 2005 and 2020. However, the supply might increase by 16%, leading to a shortage of about 2.5% in the *supply* of total active physicians in 2020.

In the case of nurses, in the United Kingdom, the "Wanless" report estimates that the demand for nurses would increase by about 25% between 2005 and 2020 and that supply would expand by a similar amount, leading to an approximate match between demand and supply in 2020.

In the United States, the HRSA has estimated in a baseline projection that the demand for nurses may increase by 31% between 2005 and 2020. A baseline estimate of supply suggested a shrinkage of 7% which would lead to a large shortage of nurses in 2020. However, the HRSA estimated that if nurse wages rose by 3% per annum between 2000 and 2020, and nurse graduates rose by 90% over the same period, supply and demand would be roughly in balance by 2020 (HSRA, 2004).

Notes

1. There are some limitations to cross-country comparability of data on physicians. In many countries, the numbers include interns and residents. The numbers are based on head counts, except in Norway which reported full-time equivalents prior to 2002. Ireland and the Netherlands report the number of all physicians entitled to practice. Data for Spain include dentists and stomatologists (OECD, 2007b).

2. In the 1980s and early 1990s, following forecasts of health workforce oversupply in Canada, United States and France, measures limiting the number of medical and nursing graduates were adopted. Recent projections suggest a shortage of health workers for the near future (Chan, 2002; Cooper *et al.*, 2002; Cash and Ulmann, 2008; HRSA, 2004; COGME, 2005).

3. The effect of ageing of the population on the rate of increase of public spending on health care has been estimated at 0.3% per annum between 1981 and 2002 (OECD, 2006b).

4. The EWTD has applied to the vast majority of employees since 1998, with a few exceptions including doctors in training. In 2004, the EWTD provisions were extended to doctors, whose maximum working hours must be reduced to 56 hours by August 2007 and to 48 hours from August 2009. Under certain undefined circumstances, national governments may apply for a further extension of a maximum of three years to delay the final reduction to 48 hours.

5. From 1 July 2003, the Accreditation Council on Graduate Medical Education has limited the working time of resident physicians to 80 hours a week. Shifts are never to last more than 24 hours, and residents will have one day off in seven and get a ten-hour break between being on call and working a shift.

6. However, nursing data reported to the OECD may be incomplete. Whereas the reductions in hospital nurses may have been counted fully, increases in nurses in domiciliary settings have gone unreported in some countries, especially if such nurses were employed in the private sector.

ISBN 978-92-64-05043-3
The Looming Crisis in the Health Workforce:
How Can OECD Countries Respond?
© OECD 2008

Chapter 2

International Recruitment and Domestic Education Policies for Human Resources for Health: Better Understanding the Interactions

Despite differences in their approach to medical and nursing education, most OECD countries exercise some form of control over student intakes. In the 1980s and 1990s, several OECD countries introduced tighter student enrolment policies with an objective of cost containment. As a result, nursing and medical graduation rates decreased. Around the turn of the last century, many OECD countries found themselves facing shortages in health workers that were partly met by increasing migration flows. The contribution of foreign-trained doctors to changes in stocks of physicians is significant and has been increasing over time in many OECD countries. There are however important cross-country differences in migration of health workers that can be explained by structural and unforeseen factors. The former reflects long standing migration trends while the latter arise from unforeseen imbalances in the health labour market, largely attributable to lags between business, political and training cycles. While international recruitments of health workers can play a role in addressing short-term shortages, in a longer term perspective there is a clear choice between using migration and other policies, such as increasing domestic training or improving productivity, to address structural imbalances between supply and demand.

Changes in the physician and nurse workforces (that is in the stocks of professionals) can be attributed to differences over time between certain key inflows to the workforce, such as registration of new graduates following domestic training, immigration and return to work following inactivity, and certain key outflows, such as retirement, emigration, temporary inactivity and death in service. Figure 2.1 depicts these inflows to and outflows from the stock in diagrammatic form.

Increasing domestic training or recruiting doctors and nurses abroad are the two most direct means to expand the health workforce. These policies have, however, quite distinct characteristics both in term of dynamics and impacts because of long education cycles and differences in the average duration of stay of migrants. For these reason, among others, OECD countries tend to choose different mixes of training and immigration. In recent years, however, international recruitment has played an increasing role in many OECD countries.

Figure 2.1. **In- and out- flows into the health workforce**

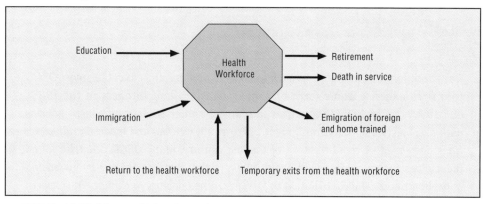

Source: OECD Health Workforce and Migration Project.

Annex B presents available data on graduation and immigration flows of foreign-trained doctors and nurses, for a selection of OECD countries in the period 1995-2005, or for sub-periods. It shows some important developments. First, whereas the number of domestic graduates was fairly flat or increasing gently in most countries over the period for which data are shown, the number of foreign-trained, physician immigrants rose sharply in most of the countries around 2002 or 2003, or earlier in Ireland, New Zealand and Norway. Secondly, including temporary employment authorisations (when data are available) immigration rates exceeded graduation rates throughout the period for which data are available in six countries (Australia, Canada, New Zealand, Norway, Switzerland and the United Kingdom) and rose above domestic graduation rates during the period in one more country (Sweden).

Data for nurses show similar trends. For example, there were upward trends in the numbers of nurse immigrants in several of the countries around the turn of the last Century. Also, numbers of foreign entrants exceeded domestic graduates in three of the countries for part of the period. However, nurse immigration appears to have played a much more modest role than physician immigration in about half of the selected countries.

These data suggest that many countries were caught by surprise fairly simultaneously, around the turn of the last Century, by a combination of rising demand and limited domestic supply; a situation which contributed to the resurgence of a questioning on "self-sufficiency" and the role of workforce planning in the health sector.

Questions such as "Do we train enough?" or "Do we need more doctors and nurses?" are certainly important, however no single answer to this question can be easily drawn for all countries because standards and targets for health professionals' density vary across countries and over time. Rather to guide policy choices, there is a need to better understand the interactions between education and migration and their contribution to health workforce supply. Before analysing the contribution of migration to changes in the health workforce in OECD countries, this chapter considers the role of education and migration policies.

1. Education of the health workforce: fluctuating training rates under control

1.1. Medical education

Despite differences across countries over medical school enrolment, virtually all OECD countries exercise some form of control over medical school intakes – often in the form of a *numerus clausus*. This is motivated by a variety of factors including: i) restrictions on entry in order to confine medical entry to the most able applicants; ii) the desire to control the total number of doctors for cost-containment reasons (because of induced-demand mechanisms); and iii) the cost of training (in all countries, including the United States, a significant part of medical education costs are publicly funded, so expansion of medical school numbers involves significant public expenditure. Controlling medical students' intake does not mean that the numbers are automatically flat or decreasing. In fact, a *numerus clausus* is instrumental to policy goals and countries have varied the cap at different times.

Annex C provides details on the different methods of control of medical and nursing student numbers adopted by OECD countries. France, Italy, Germany, Netherlands, Portugal, and more recently Belgium and some Swiss Cantons have adopted a *numerus clausus* system, whereas in New Zealand, budget constraints limit the places which are funded. Some countries, such as Ireland, leave some discretion to medical schools to determine the number of students.

Not surprisingly, countries with a high medical graduation rate like Austria, Ireland and Greece are those which have adopted more relaxed student intake policies. However, there is much variation among countries with a *numerus clausus*. While, graduation rates in Denmark and Italy are higher than OECD average, Portugal has one of the lowest medical graduation rates.

In the United States, unlike most OECD countries, the private sector plays an important role in medical education. There is no national planning, nor formal quotas or other restrictions within medical schools. The number of physicians entering the workforce is almost entirely determined by the number who completes residency training in approved programmes.[1] The Bureau of Health Professions (BHPr) and the Council on Graduate Medical Education (COGME) published projections which suggested that there would be surpluses of physicians in the 1980s and early 1990s. This led to a freeze in the expansion of medical schools. Even so, growth in demand propelled a continued expansion of the Graduate Medical Education programme partially filled by foreign-trained doctors. Many believe this was due partly to continuing financial support for the training of residents through Medicare, which is a federal programme. Medicare funding was capped in 1997. However, there is still a steady gap of approximately 25% between the number of US medical graduates and residency positions available. The additional positions are filled by international medical graduates, either US citizens[2] or foreign nationals. This is a fairly unique situation where dependence on migration is almost explicit in medical education policy (Cooper, 2008).

In Japan, which reports one of the lowest physician densities in the OECD area, the number of medical graduates per 1 000 physicians fell from 45 in 1985 to 28.5 in 2005. However, there has been almost no immigration of foreign-trained doctors into Japan. Doctor shortages have been discussed for some years and were attributed to limits on the number of medical students and the desire of the Japan Medical Association to limit competition. However, it has been reported that the Japanese government had proposed recently to increase the number of medical students – although the plan would take a long time to increase the number of doctors (Ebihara, 2007).

If annual graduation rates are expressed as a proportion of the stock of physicians, on average, graduation rates fell from about 5% to about 3% between 1985 and 2000 in 17 OECD countries for which data can be found, after which they stabilised during the following five years (Figure 2.2). The great majority of the countries concerned operated implicit or explicit controls on domestic training of physicians. The reported shortages of physicians which emerged around the turn of the last Century in many countries could not be eliminated quickly by expanding domestic training capacity. As a result part of the imbalances has been tackled through international recruitment.

Figure 2.2. **Number of medical graduates per 1 000 physicians, selected OECD countries, 1985 to 2005**

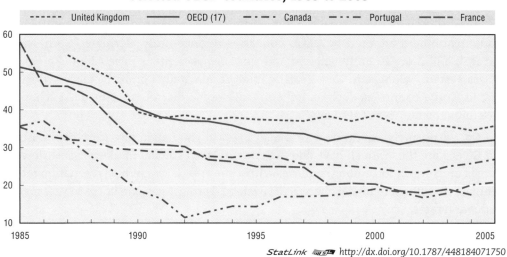

StatLink http://dx.doi.org/10.1787/448184071750

Note: Consistent average is calculated on the base of 17 OECD countries.

Source: OECD (2007b), Health at a Glance 2007, Paris.

However, domestic medical education capacity was expanded at the same time, *i.e.*, around the turn of the century, in many OECD countries. Some, like the United Kingdom (Buchan, 2008), France and Australia have increased domestic training, sometimes partly by opening new medical schools (see Box 2.1). In these countries, enrolment almost doubled between the middle of the 1990s and 2007. In Canada, there was a similar change in perception from a perceived surplus to a shortage of doctors around the mid 1990s (Barer and Stoddart, 1991). First year enrolment in Canadian Medical Schools had declined fairly steadily from about 1900 in 1983 to about 1600 in 1997. Growth resumed in 1998 and estimated enrolment was expected to be about 2400 in 2007, an increase of about 50% (Dauphinee, 2006). In the United States, the American Association of Medical

---

Box 2.1. **Changes in intakes into medical education: the not-so-contrasting examples of Australia and France**

France

In France, a dramatic change took place in the 1970s following the introduction of the *numerus clausus* in 1971 in order to contain the flow of students in medicine faculties and reduce medical density from the 1980s. While the *numerus clausus* was above 8,000 in the beginning of the 1970s, it reached a low of 3,500 in 1992 before rising again to 7 100 in 2007. The "*numerus clausus*" was introduced with the aim of avoiding an oversupply of doctors in the future. However, at that time, its level was fixed relatively high, because the discussions on the link between the number of doctors and health expenditures had only just started. Nonetheless, this issue became a central point of discussion at the end of the 1970s and resulted in the decision to lower the *numerus clausus*. This trend continued until the end of the 1990s. Medical unions, the government, and the French Social Health Insurance (Sécurité Sociale) were in favour of decreasing the number of doctors as they thought that it would allow reductions in health expenditures, while medical deans considered that such a policy would cause difficulties in hospitals where there would be insufficient interns. Based on their medical demographic projections, the French Medical Association also began to argue for increases in the *numerus clausus*, and, in the beginning the 1990's, their concern found greater echo, and since then, the *numerus clausus* has been increased on a regular basis (adapted from Cash and Ulmann, 2008).

Numerus causus in France 1972-2006

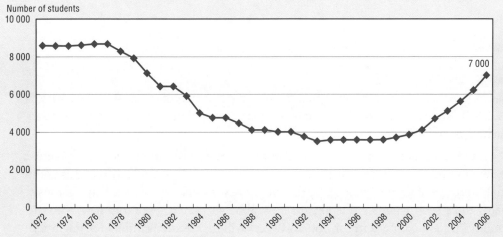

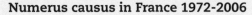
StatLink http://dx.doi.org/10.1787/448222506325

Source: Cash and Ulmann (2008).

Box 2.1. **Changes in intakes into medical education: the not-so-contrasting examples of Australia and France** (*cont.*)

Australia

"Historically, the long-term picture indicates evident cycles in Australian medical workforce supply policy, with periodic shifts between phases of containment and growth. In 1973, increases to medical school intakes were recommended in response to perceived workforce shortages. Intakes were expanded, and graduations from medical schools rose steadily during the 1970s, from 851 in 1970 to 1278 in 1980. By then, the medical workforce was believed to be in oversupply, and reductions to medical school intakes were recommended and subsequently implemented. Effects of this on graduate numbers were seen from the mid 1980s, with 1 030 graduates in 1990. The medical workforce was considered to be in surplus throughout the 1980s and into the 1990s, and medical school intakes remained static. In the late 1990s, opinion began to swing back to a view of medical workforce shortage, and after a 20-year period of no change, intakes to medical schools were once again rigorously augmented. Five new medical schools have opened since the year 2000, with a further seven programmes planned by 2008, doubling the number of medical schools since 2000. Combined with increases to intake numbers in existing medical schools, this represents a square wave shift that is in stark contrast to the static pattern of graduate numbers over the previous two decades" (Joyce *et al.*, 2007).

Australia university medical school graduates, 1970-2016

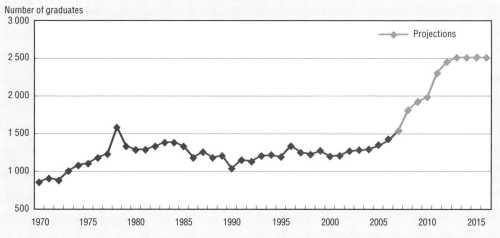

StatLink http://dx.doi.org/10.1787/448222506325

Source: Based on Joyce C., J.U. Stoelwinder, J.J. McNeil and L. Piterman (2007), "Riding the Wave: Current and Emerging Trends in Graduates from Australian University Medical Schools", *Medical Journal of Australia*, Vol. 186, p. 311.

Colleges (AAMC) called for an urgent and immediate expansion of medical schools by 30% (AAMC, 2006). By 2007, the AAMC was able to report that planned intake by its members schools was set to increase by 17% by 2012.

The rapid expansion of medical training in these countries in recent years, or planned for the near future, seems to demonstrate that OECD countries have not only recognised the potential shortages of doctors which they face but have been able to respond to it vigorously. It remains to be seen whether this expansion will be sustained,[3] whether it will lead to equilibrium in the medium term or not, and what will be the implications for migration. There have even been suggestions of possible future oversupply (Joyce *et al.*, 2007; Goodman, 2004). In at least one country, the United Kingdom, while international recruitment has helped to scale up the UK workforce rapidly, this led to an overshoot in planned targets (Buchan, 2008). There have been reports in 2007 of domestic medical graduates being unable to find postgraduate positions as junior doctors. Meanwhile, non-EU immigration of doctors and nurses into the United Kingdom has been firmly discouraged.

1.2. Nursing education

The situation for nursing schools differs to some extent as in almost half of OECD countries the training of nurses is left to decentralised market forces – a "demand driven model". Some OECD countries, nonetheless, regulate nursing school intakes (Annex C). The motivation for regulating nursing education is probably quite different from that for doctors as induced-demand mechanisms do not apply and the cost of training is more in line with other tertiary programmes. There are signs that nurse graduation fluctuated over the period 1985-2005 and declined overall in some countries (except for Australia) – although only scanty evidence is available (Figure 2.3).

Figure 2.3. **Number of nursing graduates per 1 000 nurses, selected countries, 1985 to 2005**

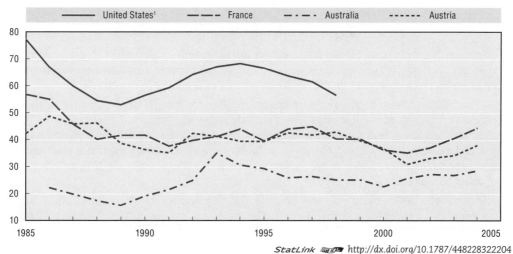

StatLink ᔄᔢᔲᔻ *http://dx.doi.org/10.1787/448228322204*

Note: Due to limitation in data availability, the OECD average is not available.
1. For the United States, the data are only available until 1998 because the data collection on licensed practical nurses graduates was discontinued afterwards.
Source: OECD (2007b), *Health at a Glance,* Paris.

In Australia, Belgium, Mexico, Netherlands, New Zealand, Norway and the United States, the number of available nursing places is determined by nursing schools themselves on the basis of student demand and their assessment of the needs of the labour market (Simoens *et al.*, 2005). The role of the government in these countries is essentially limited to the funding of public nursing education. However, in many OECD countries, the number of places available in nursing schools is planned by the government (Ministries of Health and Education) at national and/or regional level.

2. International migration of doctors and nurses

The period of rapid economic growth at the end of the 1990s, compounded by growing concerns about ageing populations, has prompted many OECD countries to consider stepping up immigration to alleviate labour shortages in general. This has contributed to putting more emphasis on skills of migrants and has persuaded most OECD countries of the need to adapt their migration policies to facilitate the international recruitment of highly-skilled workers or to adopt more selective migration policies. As part of this overall policy of encouraging skilled migration, there is now keener competition among OECD countries to attract the health care staff they lack and retain those who might emigrate. This trend comprises health workers but certainly goes well beyond the health sector (Box 2.2).

Comparing the share of foreign-born doctors or nurses to the share of foreign-born in professional occupations or PhD holders shows that migrant health professionals are generally not overrepresented (see Dumont and Zurn, 2007). The higher the percentage of foreign-born among highly-skilled workers is, the higher it is also for doctors and nurses. Similar findings are observed for expatriation rates within the OECD area.

As a result, a higher contribution of migration to changes in the health workforce could simply reflect the fact that labour migration, and more specifically highly-skilled migration, plays an important role in the dynamic of the labour market of the receiving country; a situation also influenced by language, geographic, cultural, historical as well as socio-economic factors in general.

Box 2.2. **Policies on the migration of health workers**

In most OECD countries, if not all, no migration programmes target health professionals specifically. However, general migration schemes may provide simplified procedures to facilitate the recruitment of health workers, notably at the local or regional level.

Australia and New Zealand grant special points for health professionals in their permanent migration programmes. This facilitates the immigration of health workers but only to a limited extent. In the United States, H1-B visas are available for most health professionals. In 2005, about 7 200 initial requests were approved for medicine and health occupations including 2 960 for physicians and surgeons. This corresponds to an increase of about 55% as compared to 2000.

In European OECD countries, work permits may be available for skilled immigrants and are generally granted for a limited period. These permits may be conditioned on a labour market test (*i.e.*, checks that there are no EU residents available to fill the position). Nonetheless, in most countries there are conditions under which the labour market test may be waived. This is the case, for instance, in the United Kingdom, Belgium, Ireland, Denmark, the Netherlands or Spain for occupations on the shortage list. In all these countries, all or some health professionals are, or have been included in the shortage lists.

A few OECD countries have bilateral agreements for the international recruitment of health professionals. Switzerland and Canada have a small agreement protocol which explicitly mentions health care workers and aims at facilitating the mobility between the two countries. Spain, which is supposed to have a surplus of nurses, has signed bilateral agreements, notably with France and the United Kingdom. Germany has bilateral agreements with several Central and Eastern European countries for the recruitment of foreign nursing aids. Bilateral agreements are also sometimes organised at the regional level. This is the case for instance in Italy, where several provinces have signed protocols with provinces in Romania to train and recruit nurses.

In Europe, the United Kingdom is the only country which has made intensive use of bilateral agreements and memoranda of understanding with non-OECD countries in the context of the international recruitment of doctors and nurses. It has signed an agreement with South Africa on reciprocal educational exchange of health care concepts and personnel (2003), a memorandum of understanding with India (2002) and a Protocol on Cooperation in Recruiting Health Professionals with China (2005).

2.1. Cross-country variation in migration

OECD countries are quite diverse in terms of migration. Figures 2.4 and 2.5 compare the percentage of foreign-born doctors and nurses and the emigration rates in individual OECD countries with the respective OECD unweighted averages in 2000. The Figures allocate countries into four groups according to the relative importance of their immigration and emigration of health professionals.

Figure 2.4. **Immigration and expatriation rates of health professionals (except nurses) in selected OECD countries, *circa* 2000**

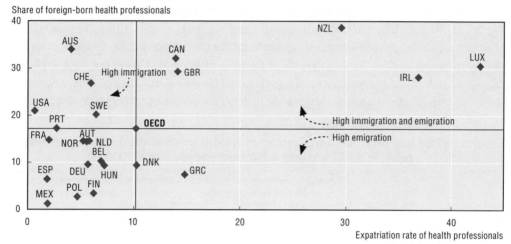

StatLink 📊 http://dx.doi.org/10.1787/448252284071

Note: Data refer to all health professionals except nurses based on ISCO (222) definition.

For each OECD country, the expatriation rate is computed by dividing the number of doctors born in that country and who are working as a doctor in another OECD country by the total number of doctors who were born in that country.

Source: Based on data from OECD (2007a), *International Migration Outlook*, Paris.

Figure 2.5. **Immigration and expatriation rates of nurses in selected OECD countries, *circa* 2000**

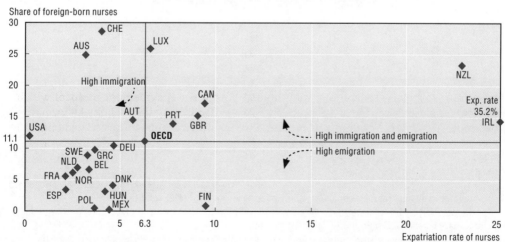

StatLink 📊 http://dx.doi.org/10.1787/448257143086

Note: Data refer to associate nurses, nursing and midwifery professionals based on ISCO (223 and 323) definition.

For each OECD country, expatriation rate is computed by dividing the number of nurses born in that country and who are working as a nurse in another OECD country by the total number of nurses who were born in that country.

Source: Based on data from OECD (2007a), *International Migration Outlook*, Paris.

Some countries like Canada, Ireland, Luxembourg, New Zealand and the United Kingdom face both important immigration and emigration of doctors and nurses. Percentages are particularly high in absolute terms for New Zealand. Conversely, Central and Eastern European countries, as well as Mexico, Turkey and Asian OECD countries were not much exposed to migration of health professionals in 2000. Countries like Australia, Switzerland and the United States appear as mainly immigration countries.

The picture drawn in Figures 2.4 and 2.5 reflects to a large extent, general migration patterns. In view of the overall importance of skilled migration in general to explain professional migration, it is necessary to control for country specific levels of highly-skilled migration to identify countries particularly reliant on migration of health professionals. Table 2.1 shows the difference in immigration and emigration of health professionals and all tertiary educated people. Negative figures indicate that migration is more important for health professionals than for highly-skilled persons in general. This is the case especially with regard to both immigration and emigration for New Zealand and Ireland, with regard to immigration for the United States, and with regard to emigration for Luxembourg.

Table 2.1. **The importance of migration of health professionals (except nurses) relative to all tertiary educated people, *circa* 2000**

	Difference in expatriation rate between tertiary educated and health professionals	Difference in the share of foreign-born between tertiary educated and health professionals.
Australia	2.1	−5.1
Austria	8.8	0.0
Belgium	−0.6	−0.1
Canada	−7.2	−6.2
Switzerland	6.5	0.9
Germany	2.3	1.5
Denmark	−3.7	−1.7
Spain	0.4	0.1
Finland	−0.3	−1.2
France	2.9	−2.4
United Kingdom	−1.2	−13.2
Greece	−6.3	4.7
Hungary	2.1	−3.5
Ireland	−13.6	−10.0
Luxembourg	−19.7	18.5
Mexico	3.8	0.1
Netherlands	2.3	−5.7
Norway	−0.3	−6.3
New Zealand	−12.2	−14.0
Poland	7.9	0.0
Portugal	8.3	−1.9
Sweden	−0.8	−5.9
United States	0.1	−7.0

StatLink http://dx.doi.org/10.1787/448315241333

Note: Data refer to all health professionals except nursing based on ISCO (222) definition.

A negative (positive) figure indicate that migration is more important for health professionals (tertiary educated) than for tertiary educated (health professionals) in general.

For each OECD country, expatriation rate is computed by dividing the number of doctors born in that country and who are working as a doctor in another OECD country by the total number of doctors who were born in that country.

Source: Based on data from OECD (2007a), *International Migration Outlook*, Paris.

Previous graphs have emphasised that in some OECD countries, for example New Zealand, Luxembourg, Ireland, immigration or emigration of health professionals represents a significant proportion of *their* total stock of health professionals. Clearly, in order to identify the impact of an individual country's policies on the global migration of health workers, the absolute number of migrants also matters (Box 2.3).

Box 2.3. **Absolute numbers also matter**

The total number of foreign-born doctors in the OECD area was about 400 000 in 2000, and the total number of foreign-born nurses was about 710 000.

The United States is the main receiving country within the OECD with about 200 000 foreign-born doctors and 280 000 foreign-born nurses, *circa* 2000 (the corresponding figures for the foreign-trained were about the same as for doctors and roughly half as much for nurses). The second largest receiving countries in the OECD are the United Kingdom for doctors with about 50 000 foreign-born doctors and Germany for nurses with at least 75 000 foreign-born nurses.

This means that the United States received 47% of the total number of foreign-born doctors in the OECD in 2000. The OECD-EU25 countries received approximately 39% of all foreign-born doctors working in the OECD area, although a significant proportion of the foreign-born in the European Union originate from within the European Union (about 24% for doctors and 38% for nurses). Australia and Canada received each close to 5% of the total. The breakdown by destination country for nurses is quite similar.

More data and analysis on the absolute and relative number of foreign-trained and foreign-born doctors and nurses across OECD countries is available from Dumont and Zurn (2007).

2.2. *The role of migration in shaping the health workforce*

The information based on place of birth could give a distorted image of the role of international migration in shaping the health workforce in OECD countries if a significant share of foreign-born health professionals were in fact trained in the receiving country and not in their origin country. A comparison between foreign-born and foreign-trained health professionals in OECD countries indicates lower percentages for the latter than for the former (Dumont and Zurn, 2007). While in countries where people tend to migrate at a young age data on the foreign-trained are a better indicator of professional migration than data on the foreign-born, this is not always the case. For example, in Finland the foreign-trained are often Finnish-born citizens who were trained abroad (notably in Sweden). Even in the United States, a growing number of foreign-trained intakes into post-graduate medical training are US citizens who undertook their initial medical training abroad.

To better identify the role of migration, variations in the stock of foreign-trained doctors between 1970-2005, 1995-2005 and 2000-2005, can be compared to that of the total stock of doctors in selected OECD countries. Figure 2.6 depicts important differences between countries, with Switzerland and Ireland having the largest reliance on international recruitments over the past five years. In the United Kingdom and in the United States, about 50% of the increase in the stock of doctors may be related to changes in the stock of foreign-trained doctors between 2000 and 2005. Important percentages are also found for France and to a lesser extent for New Zealand and Sweden.[4]

Figure 2.6. **Contribution of the foreign-trained doctors to the net increase in the number of practicing doctors in selected OECD countries**

Percentage 1970-2005

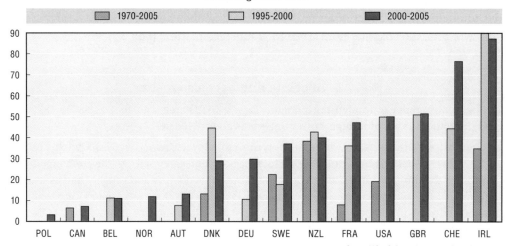

StatLink ⌦ http://dx.doi.org/10.1787/448315565273

Note: Data for Germany, Belgium and Norway refer to foreign doctors instead of foreign-trained doctors.

Source: OECD Health Data 2007 and OECD (2007a), International Migration Outlook, Paris.

In spite of cross country differences, in all countries for which data are available, migration played a more important role in shaping the medical workforce over the past ten years than it has, on average, since the 1970s. The increase is particularly marked in Ireland, France and the United States but negligible in New Zealand and Canada.

Data for nurses are only available for a few countries but show similar trends. For instance, foreign-trained nurses account for most of the increase of the total stock of nurses in Ireland between 2000 and 2005. The situation is even more striking in New Zealand where, ceteris paribus, the total number of nurses would have declined markedly without immigration (Zurn and Dumont, 2008). In the United States, the percentage of foreign-trained registered nurses in the total of newly registered nurses has doubled between 1995 and 2006 (Aiken and Cheung, 2008). The contribution of foreign-trained nurses to the total number of nurses was also important in Ireland, Denmark and Canada. For other countries where data are available (Belgium, Sweden, Finland and the Netherlands) the role of migration is more limited.

2.3. Why and when international recruitment of health professionals takes place

Many factors contribute to explain cross-country differences in the contribution of migration to changes in health workforce stocks. In some cases international recruitment of doctors and nurses will result from unforeseen mismatch between supply and demand for doctors or nurses but, as already discussed, it could also be the case that they simply reflect the role of migration in the dynamic of the labour market in general.

Unforeseen mismatch between supply and demand due to exogenous shocks

Despite the efforts devoted by national and regional authorities to anticipate and control the demand for health professionals, the inflow of new graduates may be insufficient to meet demand. This can occur primarily because of the length of medical education:[5] it takes about ten years to train a doctor, which may be far more than for government policy to change.

Legislative changes with respect to working hours for junior doctors or other health professionals in general, notably in the EU context with the Working Time Directive but also in the United States, are good examples of unanticipated demand shocks which have contributed to unbalance the health labour market.

A large and sustained rise in public spending on the NHS, a few years after the election of the Labour Party in the United Kingdom in 1997, provides another straightforward example of a sudden change in demand for health professionals. Despite the fact that the NHS adopted an ambitious mixed strategy to achieve staff growth, including increasing training, improving retention and fostering return to the workforce, in the short run, international recruitment had to be increased significantly to respond to the needs (see Buchan, 2007 and 2008). As a result, foreign-trained doctors employed by the NHS in England increased from about 22 000 in 1997 to almost 39 000 in 2005.

Difficulties in responding to the demand for health workers can also result from unexpected outflows from the health workforce, including emigration. The EU enlargement in 2004 and 2007 has affected the inflows of foreign doctors and nurses from new accession countries. This provides a good example of the potential of external shocks to impact the health workforce of origin countries. In a different context, New Zealand and, to a lesser extent Canada, Ireland or the United Kingdom, which receive and send lots of doctors and nurses abroad, may be at mercy of sudden policy changes in other OECD countries which remain beyond their control.

Exogenous technological innovation may also impact the demand for health workers as it creates needs for new health-care services (*e.g.* the development of Magnetic Resonance Imaging) or changes in care delivery and skill mix. Finally, many OECD countries, despite a combination of incentives and regulatory measures, face persisting difficulties in matching the geographic distribution and/or specialty distribution of health professionals with that of the needs of the population.[6] As a result, unmet demand may occur in local areas or in specific occupations even if the overall supply of health workers may be, in theory, sufficient to address the needs.

There are certainly many reasons for unforeseen mismatches between demand and supply of health workers to occur and in many of these cases migration often emerges as the leading short-term adjustment variable, probably before prices or wages which are usually controlled for a variety of reasons.

Difficulties in health workforce planning

Health workforce planning is advocated by many to facilitate the attainment of an "adequate" supply of health personnel. In fact, all OECD countries undertake some form of health workforce planning but these exercises face a number of difficulties (Kolars, 2001).

First, fixing numerical limits essentially supposes a solid capacity to anticipate future demand. This seldom proves to be an easy task and there are many examples of prophecies of shortages or over-supply which never materialise. Uncertainties related to future population health needs, technological progress, as well as methodological sensitivity altogether contribute to weaken forecasting exercises. As a result, health workforce planning may at best serve as a broad-brush tool.

Secondly, health workforce planning in OECD countries can be biased by a potential "free rider" phenomenon. Countries have inadequate incentives to train sufficient health workers so long as they can rely on immigration to fill any gaps between supply and demand. Also, training more health professionals than necessary may be costly in terms of public expenditure. The resulting temptation is to risk shortages and to export them, if they arise.

Third, a lack of coordination across different areas of planning may be an impediment.[7] In the United Kingdom, the recent report on workforce planning by the House of Commons called for a better integration between workforce, financial and services planning (House of Commons, 2007).

Fourth, the places in university medical and nursing programmes may be limited or reduced in light of budgetary constraints, limited availability of teachers and inadequate teaching capacity. Italy experiences a growing nurses' crisis. The places in nursing programmes have been increasing at 2% annually since 2000, yet budget cuts have prevented the creation of more nursing care positions, resulting in a nursing care shortage (Chaloff, 2008). Similar failures of static supply to match growing demand have occurred in other OECD countries.

Finally, while workforce planning could represent a promising area to consider the dynamic between domestic training and international recruitments, this is rarely the case. Immigration and emigration flows are seldom fully taken into account, except by assuming constant figures. This is a major shortcoming as inflows of foreign medical students and of foreign-trained health professionals are making an increasing contribution to the health workforce in many OECD countries, as seen above.

Determinants of migration of health professionals

Not all the migration of health professionals should be regarded as responding to pull factors specific to the health sector of the destination country – such as better pay, professional development and career opportunities, or a desire to work in a diverse environment. Many other factors play a role, including push factors in the origin country, as well as migration policies (Box 2.4).

2.4. Limits of international recruitment of health workers

International recruitment of foreign-trained health workers is not a *panacea*, even if it might help to adjust supply to demand in the short run and may contribute to reducing the costs of training for the recruiting country. Significant limitations to relying on immigration for particular countries include: problems related to the integration of immigrants into health workforce (such as the recognition of foreign qualifications and language proficiency); costs of international recruitment, especially when migration is mainly temporary; difficulties in retaining doctors and nurses in less attractive locations and positions; and the risk of becoming excessively dependent on foreign health professionals to fill domestic needs.

Long-term retention will be particularly problematic if the key reason for recruitment lies in domestic supply shortages, and outflows from the profession are due to relatively poor professional employment and working conditions in the receiving country. Some nursing recruitment is often alleged to occur for this reason. Systematic recourse to immigration might discourage domestic responses such as increasing training and creating adequate incentives to join the health profession. That might induce further reliance on migration inflows.

Box 2.4. **Modelling the determinants of the contribution of foreign-trained doctors to the health workforce**

Different sets of covariates of the contribution of foreign-trained doctors to changes in stock of physicians for 1995-2000 and 2000-2005 have been considered, including indicators of education (*numerus clausus*, current and lagged graduation rates), health expenditures (as a percentage of GDP and growth rate), variation in the number of doctors (growth rate and increase in the number of practicing doctors) as well as migration (expatriation rate of doctors and percentage of foreign-born among the highly skilled).

While this tentative exercise faces a number of limitations due to data availability, it confirms the predominant role of the general context of migration in explaining the relative importance of international recruitments of doctors in shaping the health workforce. Also, countries facing a higher expatriation rate of their doctors tend to recruit more abroad. The relative importance of highly-skilled migration in general explains a significant part of cross-country differences. In fact, this variable has a coefficient close to one but not very significant in the estimated equation below:

$$Share\_FT\_Doc = 3.4 + 0.4 \cdot P9500 + 1.2 \cdot Share\_FB\_HS + 1.7 \cdot Expatriation\_rate$$
$$(9.3) \quad (7.2) \qquad (0.6) \qquad * \qquad (0.6) \qquad ***$$

$$N = 32 \quad R^2 adj. = 0.31 \quad *** = 1\% \quad * = 10\%$$

Where:

Share_FT_Doc = Percentage of the change in stock of physicians attributable to changes in stock of foreign-trained doctors

P9500 = Index for the period 1995-2000

Expatriation rate = Expatriation rate of doctors (2000)

Share_FB_HS = Share of the persons with tertiary education who are foreign born (2000)

However, no robust evidence of the impact of other indicators (*e.g.*, variation in the number of doctors, education, health expenditure) can be identified. This does not mean that there is no link but rather that it probably goes both ways: i) important growth in the stock of doctors is recorded when investments in education have been made several years before, implying no further need to recruit abroad; and ii) sudden changes in the demand for doctors result in more migration.

It is particularly difficult to disentangle the main determinants of the contribution of foreign-trained doctors to variations in the total stock of doctors with cross country data because much of the relationship probably lies in idiosyncratic effects that could only be considered with panel data.

Data are available for only two periods (1995-2000 and 2000-2005) for 16 OECD countries (32 observations) and do not include any qualitative indicators on health policy or migration policy. In particular, longitudinal data are lacking to identify country-specific effects.

Notes

1. Undergraduate medical education is however partly funded by states, notably through Medicaid. About 60% of all allopathic medical schools and 30% of osteopathic medical schools are state owned or state related.

2. Between 1985 and 2000, approximately 1 000 US-IMGs entered residency training annually, a number that has increased in recent years, largely because of the growth of medical schools in the Caribbean (Cooper, 2008).

3. For example, this is due to cost. The cost of expansion still appears to be a debated issue in the United States. The annual investment necessary to reach the objective of the AAMC to expand by 30% medical school enrolment is estimated between USD 4 and USD 5 billion (Weiner, 2007).

4. In some countries, like the United States, the percentages computed are higher than what would have been suggested if the analysis was based on flow data on immigration. This is because foreign-trained doctors tend to be permanent immigrants in the United States and are underrepresented in workforce outflows. Few of them depart and most of the retirees are in age cohorts which included few foreign-trained doctors. In other countries, such as New Zealand or the United Kingdom, the opposite can be observed, as migration is mainly temporary, but also because emigration of home trained doctors is quite important. Emigration is also significant for Germany. In the case of France the importance of migration is essentially explained by decreasing (and low) graduation rates since at least the past two decades despite a sustained increase in the total number of doctors

5. The situation is to some extent different for nurses, although Specialised Registered Nurses (*e.g.* operating theatre nurse, nurse anesthetist, emergency nurse, oncology nurse, etc.) also need to follow a lengthy training process.

6. See Section 1.5 in Chapter 3 for a discussion about the potential role of migration in addressing geographic imbalances.

7. Workforce planning also often ignores the interrelationship between health professions (Maynard, 2006).

ISBN 978-92-64-05043-3
The Looming Crisis in the Health Workforce:
How Can OECD Countries Respond?
© OECD 2008

Chapter 3

Better Use and Mobilisation of Workforce Skills

Chapter 3 reviews other health workforce policies aiming at an efficient use of the available health resources. A better use and mobilisation of available health workforce skills is possible through a portfolio of policies, including: improving retention, enhancing integration, developing more efficient skill mix, and improving productivity.

Oecd countries can adopt a variety of policies to make better use of the *existing* health workforce to address future shortages. Better retention, enhanced integration, and a more efficient skill-mix within the existing workforce can contribute to improving their availability, competence, responsiveness and productivity. Furthermore a country will more easily retain its existing health professionals when its health workforce is managed well and thus will have less need for recourse to additional immigration, *ceteris paribus*. This is why a combination of all policies is desirable for successfully addressing health workforce shortages. Policies to make better use of the existing workforce will be reviewed in this chapter.

1. Retaining the health workforce

Each year, many health workers move to a different position or leave, temporarily or permanently, the profession, the region or the country.[1] To reduce turnover,[2] policy makers and health-system managers have often increased remuneration and employed financial incentives. However, the impact of these practices is mixed. Alternative policies focusing on improving occupational status and the working environment are gaining increasing attention and appear to produce good results.

1.1. Retention difficulties compromise the ability to deliver high-quality care

While a certain degree of turnover is to be expected in an efficient medical and nursing labour market, excessive turnover might compromise the delivery of high quality health services and signal retention difficulties. It generates recruitment and temporary replacement costs, and it is associated with initial low productivity among the new hires. For example, O'Brien-Pallas and colleagues estimated the direct and indirect cost of turnover per nurse at USD 16 600 in Australia, USD 10 100 in Canada, USD 10 200 in New Zealand and at USD 33 000 in the United States (O'Brien-Pallas *et al.*, 2006). Retention difficulties can also negatively affect a number of important treatment and follow-up activities (Minore *et al.*, 2005).

Different types of turnover will call for a diversity of policy approaches to managing retention. "Controlled" turnover refers to retirement, redundancy and redeployment. "Voluntary" turnover is used to refer to employees leaving in response to dissatisfaction in the current job or to seek career progression and better pay in a new job. Unfortunately, there is no systematic information on the relative importance of each type of turnover. Some evidence suggests that retirement and voluntary termination are among the main drivers of turnover, although there is substantial variation across countries and professions (O'Brian-Pallas *et al.*, 2007; Cash and Ulmann, 2008).

1.2. Is it all about better pay?

There are a number of financial levers to assist managers and policy makers to retain medical and nursing staff, including pay rises, bonuses, loan-repayment policies, targeted financial aid for staff families, and training scholarships.

Improved remuneration is among the most common approaches to reduce nurse turnover. Yet, financial incentives have produced mixed results here. While between 58% and 90% of nurses in several European countries express significant dissatisfaction with pay, evidence from one of the NEXT studies[3] suggests that poor remuneration explains only marginally their intention to leave the nursing profession. Literature reviews on nursing supply found only a weak positive relationship between wage and labour supply (Shield, 2004; Chiha and Link, 2003; and Antonazzo *et al.*, 2003). However, there is some evidence that wage is one underlying reason for leaving the profession (Hasselhorn *et al.*, 2005).

Setting the right remuneration level to influence doctors' supply is far from easy. Health sector reforms aiming at keeping remuneration from rising in order to contain overall health cost have exposed some countries to difficulties in maintaining an adequate level of services (Docteur and Oxley, 2004). Pay increases for doctors in the United Kingdom, implemented as part of a new contract for hospital consultants in 2003, seem to have increased consultant numbers (Buchan, 2008). But they also led to significant cost increase (NAO, 2007). As in the case of nurses, policies have focused on a mix of both financial and other incentives, such as on improving working-time flexibility, creating more flexible career development opportunities and offering a wider range of options for continued education and training.

1.3. *Better workforce organisation and working conditions*

Low esteem, limited work control and dissatisfaction[4] with working conditions seem to be more important determinants of decisions to leave the nursing profession than perceived low pay (Hasselhorn *et al.*, 2005). As a result, policies focusing on the occupational status and the working environment are gaining increasing attention. Several OECD countries have developed policies to reduce nurse turnover by alleviating workload (Simoens *et al.*, 2005). Healthy workplace' strategies such as flexible work arrangements, family-friendly initiatives, leave and compensation benefits and safety practices are perceived to have a positive impact on nurse retention (Wagner *et al.*, 2002). Other successful initiatives include career development programmes and job redesign or task-shifting to reduce burnout. A study on the perceived work ability of nurses in ten European countries suggests institutional policies to sustain work ability through better working conditions, improving quality of the working environment and finding suitable alternative nursing work for those no longer able to cope in their current post (Camarino *et al.*, 2006).

The so-called "magnet hospitals" in the United States offer examples of successful practices. Magnet hospitals typically adopt: flat organisational structure, decentralised decision-making, flexibility in scheduling, positive nurse-physician relationships, opportunities for professional development, a good balance between effort and reward, and investment in education for nurses (Hasselhorn *et al.*, 2005). These institutions have successfully attracted and retained nurses during times of serious shortages, while also achieving good patient outcomes. The number of hospitals that have achieved or applied for Magnet Recognition for organisational excellence in nursing services administration suggests positive changes have been achieved in US nurse work environments (Aiken and Cheung, 2008).

Although retention is less critical an issue for doctors than it is for nurses, workforce strategies addressing non-monetary factors appear likewise to affect physician retention. According to one recent study on Germany, three factors have a direct impact on physicians' job satisfaction and hence retention, namely decision-making and recognition; continuous education and job security; administrative tasks and collegial relationships (Janus *et al.*, 2007).

Flexibility is an important factor, especially given the growing feminisation of the medical workforce (Figure 1.6 above). Young and Leese (1999) identified improving working-time flexibility, creating more flexible career development opportunities, and offering a wider range of options for continued education as the main instruments to improve medical retention in the United Kingdom. Moreover, there are gender-related differences in the content of work and choice of medical specialisations, requiring policy attention in light of the transition from a traditionally male profession to an increasingly female profession. Organisational changes might however be difficult to implement. Introducing flexible working hours or increasing work autonomy is likely to meet some resistance and face bureaucratic difficulties in many organisations. There can also be country-specific difficulties. Part-time employment opportunities exist in the United States, including opportunities for older physicians, but the high costs of malpractice insurance, which are not pro-rated for part-time employment, often present a barrier (Cooper, 2008).

Finally, violence against health professionals, in particular women, is a growing phenomenon[5] which has however not captured much attention so far (Dalphond et al., 2000). Some studies suggest a direct link between aggression and the increases in sick leave, burnout and staff turnover (Farrell, 1999; O'Connel et al., 2000). Initiatives to reduce violence have started to appear in some OECD countries. In the United Kingdom, the National Health Service initiated a *Zero Tolerance* campaign in 1999 – later replaced by the Security Management Service – to better protect NHS staff and property. Among the most common measures implemented to reduce violence are the introduction of closed circuit television surveillance, controlled access to certain areas, security guards, and better lighting.

1.4. *Improving retention in remote and underserved areas*

Virtually all OECD countries suffer from a geographical maldistribution of their health workforce between rural, remote or poor areas and urban, central, and rich localities. The largest disparities in doctors per capita between the best and least-endowed regions are found in the United States and in Turkey, where the regions with the highest densities may have up to 2.5 and 2.2 times the national average, respectively (Figure 3.1). Unfortunately, data on regional variation in staffing levels are not adjusted for need, making it impossible to judge to what extent differences may reflect variation across areas with unequal needs.

Financial incentives to improve geographical maldistribution of doctors seem to generate mixed results. Wage differences are one of the most frequent reasons for international migration, especially between lower and higher income countries (WHO, 2006). Domestic programmes offering higher remuneration for doctors and nurses locating or moving to underserved, deprived, or rural areas tend to have a short-term impact, but no lasting effect in the medium to long term (Bourgueil et al., 2006) possibly because wage payments alone cannot compensate for lack of facilities and for lack of access to good education for doctors' and nurses' families. Similar issues arise in middle income countries, notably South Africa. It is also unclear whether pay-related policies are more or less costly than other educational or regulatory approaches (Simoens and Hurst, 2006).

As in the case of financial incentives, many of the policies to address geographical imbalances have tended to have only a short term impact. Australia, the United States and New Zealand have developed minimum-stay requirements for immigrant doctors or locum programmes and visa waivers to attract foreign health professionals to underserved areas. Moreover, though migrant health workers are indeed willing to address problems of maldistribution and undersupply, few appear to be retained in areas of need once

Figure 3.1. **Regional variations in physician density**

Percentages of national average, 2004

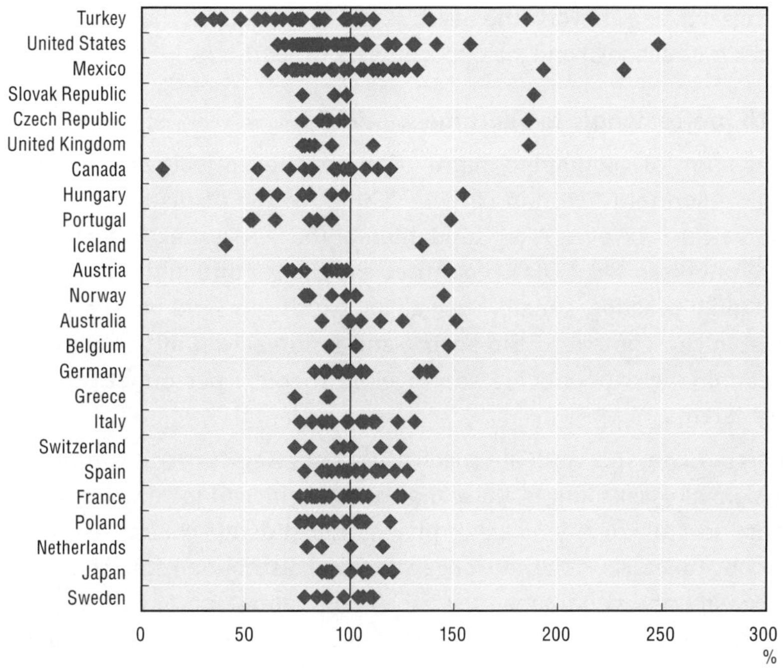

StatLink ᵐᵇᵖ http://dx.doi.org/10.1787/448322242421

Note: Each point above refers to the density of doctors in one particular region relative to the average density in the corresponding country. Regions located under (resp. over) 100% have a density of doctors which is lower (resp. higher) than the national average.

Source: OECD (2007c), *Regions at a Glance*, Paris.

permanent status and/or unconstrained registration has been achieved, a pattern ensuring that fresh global intakes are regularly required. Also, large short-term inflows do not allow the continuity of practice in the medium to long term, and have high turnover cost in terms of recruitment and training.

Increasingly, OECD countries have adopted measures to improve medium and long-term retention in rural areas. They have encouraged student interest in working in rural areas during basic training, or improved professionals' skills for working in these areas, or better identified students most apt to work in rural areas. Students originating from remote areas are more likely to go back to practice in their origin regions. Recently, New Zealand medical schools have increased their entry quota to allow more students from rural areas in medical schools. In Canada, medical school training has largely been conducted in urban areas, and has offered only limited, optional, exposures to rural medicine and lifestyle. Hence, efforts have been undertaken in three specific areas regarding education and medical training. These include providing more exposure to rural medicine in medical schools, developing rural relevant skills in residency, and increasing the number of medical students from rural areas. The expansion of the undergraduate medical education in British Columbia and the founding of a new medical school in Northern Ontario, both with campuses in rural areas, illustrate this new approach regarding exposure to rural medicine and lifestyle (Dumont and Zurn, 2008).

Policies have also sought to prevent isolation of health professionals and to improve lifestyle. They have included measures to encourage collaboration and coordination between health professionals in rural areas, facilitate professional development, and help spouses to find a job (Bourgueil *et al.*, 2006). However, addressing staffing shortages in underserved areas requires a mix of policies which go beyond the heath sector. For example, these areas do not offer minimum services (*e.g.,* schools) and job opportunities for partners.

1.5. Attracting health professionals to shortage specialties

Similar to the question of geographic distribution are the difficulties in recruiting medical and nursing personnel to certain careers. The question of distribution across specialities may in some cases be even more fundamental that the issue of shortages and surpluses in aggregate numbers. Most OECD countries experience difficulties in attracting medical students to family practice, general specialists, psychiatry, and other specialties needed in rural areas. In the context of the ageing and feminisation of the population, some OECD countries may be experiencing shortages in medical personnel trained for geriatrics and surgery careers.

Even when undergraduate and graduate medical and nursing curricula are promptly adapted in light of epidemiological changes, these may not be sufficient to attract students to certain careers, because several conditions are at play in the students' choice – status, pay, perceived burden, working times. As in the case of geographical distribution, improvements to relative pay, work flexibility and conditions of service and suppression of bullying during training may be necessary to attract doctors to less popular specialties. For example, these appear critical for encouraging women to undertake a career in surgery (Ormanczyk *et al.*, 2002). Early career advice and support during medical school and after graduation was found to encourage young doctors to take up shortage specialties in the United Kingdom (Mahoney *et al.*, 2004). According to a review of experience in OECD countries, giving students experience of primary care practice and appointing primary-care role models to academic positions influence students' choices towards a career in primary care (Simoens and Hurst, 2006).

1.6. Developing flexible retirement policies

In many countries the "baby boom" generation account for a substantial share of the workforce, and many will reach retirement age within the next ten to twenty years. Until recently, few OECD countries had implemented or planned specific policies to address this issue (Simoens *et al.*, 2005). In fact, until the late 1990s, it was common cost-saving strategy for employers in some countries to offer early-retirement incentives to nurses.[6] The feminisation of the medical workforce is likely to reinforce these trends, as women health professionals tend to retire earlier than their male counterparts.[7] In some OECD countries, the yearly number of retirees has already been close to that of graduates and retirement rates will increase in the future.[8]

More flexible working patterns that allow health professionals who have reached pensionable age to continue to work and receive pension benefits may encourage them to delay retirement. In the United Kingdom, a flexible-retirement initiative launched in 2000 enabled staff nearing retirement to move into part-time work while preserving pension entitlements (Simoens and Hurst, 2006). In France, doctors who reach the statutory pensionable age can combine a pension and earnings up to an income limit. Also, elderly doctors can be exempted from night and week-end shifts (Cash and Ulmann, 2008). In Belgium, a number of hospitals have experienced better nurse retention by allowing those aged 55 years and older to work 32 hours while still earning the wage corresponding to 40 hours (Peterson, 2001).

Strategies to improve retention should address modification of the mix of tasks performed by "older nurses". In Canada, for example, nurses have one of the highest sick-leave rates of all workers. These are mainly attributed to work-induced stress, burnout and musculoskeletal injury, which are likely to affect older nurses in particular (Shamian et al., 2003).

Finally, many OECD countries are debating changes in the statutory pensionable age. While such an approach could contribute to alleviate shortages to some extent, this measure, if adopted, will take time for it to take full effect. Also, this will not reduce the rate of pre-retirement withdrawal from the profession.

2. Enhancing integration in the health workforce

Immigrant health workers who cannot practice their profession in the destination country and doctors and nurses dropping out of the health labour market (other than those reaching retirement age) represent a loss of skills. OECD countries might benefit from addressing the process of recognition of the diploma of foreign-trained health professionals, as well as from designing policies to recruit back domestically-trained health workers who have left the workforce.

2.1. Recognition of foreign diplomas and targeting errors

As a prerequisite for practice, health professionals must meet registration or licensing requirements. This guarantees the educational and practice standards which are needed to promote patient safety and high quality of health care delivery. To obtain registration, foreign-trained doctors and nurses must obtain recognition of their qualifications. Recognition procedures are necessary to ensure that practice standards are met when foreign professionals are absorbed into the health workforce. However, they may also serve as a means to control unwanted inflows of foreign-trained health workers. Despite common features, OECD countries have adopted somewhat different approaches towards such recognition (Box 3.1).

The process of recognising foreign qualifications is complex and can lead to significant inefficiencies due to errors in targeting.

A first important inefficiency, although not discussed in depth in this report, concerns accepting qualifications which are invalid. The quality of medical and nursing education is not homogenous and this limits the cross-transferability of skills. Errors in this direction risk endangering patients' safety and, ultimately, would damage health outcomes. Much of the delays, rejections, and scrupulous screening involved in the process of recognition of foreign qualifications have to do with preventing these errors. Clearly, other policy objectives may play a role in the process, too. For example delays in recognition may be shortened or criteria relaxed depending on the state of the domestic job market, as emerges from the experience of the United Kingdom (Buchan, 2007). Language proficiency, although not directly related to professional skills, is also a key requirement for responsive, efficient and safe delivery of health care. Migrants need to satisfy language tests in most OECD countries and in some cases the passing scores have been increased recently (Box 3.1).

Second, rejecting (or failing to recognise) qualifications which are valid may induce qualified health professionals to work in low-pay or low-skill occupations, below their level of qualification. This loss of social status and, often, financial resources, can produce lower motivation for health professionals and difficulties in societal integration. It also produces a

---

Box 3.1. Approaches to the recognition of foreign qualifications

After verifying credentials, health professionals need to satisfy language tests, and theoretical and practical licensing exams. For example, the national licensing examination for registered nurses in the United States, or the registration examination (the NZREX clinical) for doctors in New Zealand. In some countries, for instance in New Zealand or the United Kingdom, the required level of language proficiency has been increased over time, which can have a direct impact on inflows of foreign-trained doctors and nurses. A period of adaptation or initial supervision is required in the United Kingdom, Finland and Ireland.

Requirements tend to be less restrictive and recognition of qualifications is facilitated within free mobility areas (*e.g.*, the Nordic Passport Union, the Trans-Tasman Area, the European Union). For example, under the legal framework adopted by the European Union, medical professionals' training certificates obtained in one member state are recognised automatically in other member states.

Some OECD countries adopt simplified procedures leading to temporary or conditional registration of health professionals, for example when skills are considered as near-equivalent (the Netherlands) or when health professionals entered the country as temporary migrants and through sponsoring schemes (Australia). In New Zealand, provisional registration is offered to individuals who worked continuously for at least three years in a health system considered as comparable (Zurn and Dumont, 2008).

At the other end of the scale, some countries require foreign-trained professionals to obtain national postgraduate qualifications (*e.g.*, Canada); complete internship periods and postgraduate residency training (*e.g.*, the United States); or to acquire citizenship of the host country (*e.g.*, Italy, Finland, Greece, Turkey and Luxembourg). In France, despite the fact that the Public Health Code mentions a criterion of nationality (Art. L-4111-1), in practice many foreign doctors are working in public hospitals. Most of them used to be working under precarious contract arrangements as trainees. An important effort has been made recently to regularise their professional status (about 9 500 authorisations have been delivered by the Health Ministry since 1999), and a new procedure has been implemented for recognition of qualifications of foreign-trained doctors (Ordre National des Médecins, 2006). These requirements delay entry or reduce inflows of foreign-trained professionals into the health workforce of the host country.

---

waste of qualified skills in need in the health sector. Many health professionals immigrate on grounds other than their professional skills (refugees, family members) and failure to use their skills is a clear loss. Unfortunately, little evidence is available on the scope of this *brain waste* in the medical field and even more on its economic impact. Calculations of the cost of non-recognition of foreign credentials are complex and, where available, their validity is affected by measurement difficulties and assumptions about the transferability of diploma and quality of education in origin countries (von Zweck and Burnett, 2006; Reitz, 2001).

Strategies to ease integration difficulties

Several countries have employed specific programmes to facilitate the integration of foreign-trained health professionals. The Canadian government has recently allocated CAD 75 million to fully integrate 1 000 physicians and 500 other health care professionals who move permanently to Canada in the next five years, while Australia has funded competency-based bridging programmes for the past 20 years, achieving highly efficient outcomes in nursing (Hawthorne, 2006; Hawthorne *et al.*, 2006). The Canadian government has also invested in efforts to streamline the process for verifying the credentials of international medical graduates, and has enhanced access to information by creating a national database about international medical graduates. In Portugal, a relatively small programme supported by non-governmental organisations assists immigrant nurses in obtaining the equivalence of their educational and professional diploma.

Refugees face particular difficulties in having their medical qualification recognised, notably because of lack of language proficiency and absence of relevant documents. The United Kingdom has implemented special programmes to help refugees and overseas qualified health professionals who are settled in the United Kingdom to pass qualification requirements (Butler and Eversley, 2005). Similar initiatives exist in the United States and other OECD countries (Dumont and Zurn, 2007).

Policies have also addressed social factors and practices that militate against the integration and retention of foreign-born health professionals into society and work (Box 3.2). These programmes facilitate the integration of immigrants and internationally trained health professionals into the labour force, although no evaluation of their cost effectiveness is available.

Box 3.2. Retention of foreign-born health professionals

While there is no reason why foreign-trained health workers should behave any differently from domestic trained health workers, in practice they often face specific difficulties that might contribute to recruitment and retention problems.

Social and cultural factors may play a role in the retention of overseas nurse graduates (Omeri, 2006). In the United Kingdom, for example, foreign-trained nurses encounter language problems, are confronted with differences in clinical and technical skills, and may face open racism in the workplace (Buchan, 2004). Many may choose to change job or re-migrate.

In some cases, existing practices may make it more difficult for foreign-born professionals to remain in the labour market. For example, contractual arrangements with foreign-trained health workers might be used to fill in temporary shortages or address turnover. In other cases, contractual arrangements may improve retention. In the United States, some hospitals contract agencies to recruit foreign-trained nurses and will benefit from the agency's insurance or full or partial remuneration if recruited nurses fail their contractual obligation (Brush *et al.*, 2004).

Most countries do not have specific retention policies for foreign health workers, even when the latter represent a large share of the health workforce. Policies aiming at matching skills, improving language knowledge, and helping migrants in their new social and cultural environment could thus be very beneficial. Some public institutions hire private companies to address some of these issues. For instance, the Royal Danish Armed Forces contracted a private company to recruit doctors from Poland. In this process, intensive Danish language training as well as professional and cultural adaptation is provided during several months before doctors start working in Denmark (Paragona, 2006).

2.2. Recruiting "back" health workers

Evidence on policies to "recruit back" health workers who have left the health profession is rather scarce. However, some recent experience suggests that such policies could make a difference. This has given rise to growing policy interest on the topic. While the potential to recruit back doctors seems limited in most OECD countries because the number of inactive doctors is relatively small, the pool of inactive nurses is larger (Gupta *et al.*, 2003).

In New Zealand, for instance, around 14% of the Registered Nurses (RN) and Midwives in 2000[9] were neither in a nursing or midwifery job, nor in paid employment. This percentage was even higher for enrolled nurses (NZHIS, 2002). In the United States, almost 17% of licensed Registered Nurses[10] were not employed in nursing as of 2004 (USDHHS, 2006). This was the lowest percentage of inactivity since 1980, but it represents nonetheless a significant outflow from the nurse stock (Aiken and Cheung, 2008). Although almost 40% of these inactive nurses were aged 60 years or above – and thus did not have good prospects for returning to active employment – the potentially employable group of RNs below the age of 50 totalled approximately 160 000 individuals. Considering the total number of vacant positions for Registered Nurses in hospitals of around 116 000 (AHA, 2007), policies to attract back nurses would seem to have a high potential.

Given the cost of training nurses, it is likely that the benefit of policies to recruit back nurses would more than outweigh cost. Furthermore, a relatively large percentage of inactive nurses seem to be interested in returning to practice. In New Zealand, for example, over three quarters of inactive nurses and midwives would consider returning to clinical work (Zurn and Dumont, 2008).

However, few countries have developed specific policies to attract nurses back to the profession and, where implemented, strategies have not proved an easy task. In the United Kingdom, the National Health Service Plan encouraged the return of qualified nurses by providing back-to-practice courses, improved work-based learning, additional nursery facilities, and mentoring of nurses returning to work (Secretary of State for Health, 2000). Over the past few years, the annual number of nurses and midwife returnees is estimated around 3 800 or 1% of the total number of qualified nurses and midwives, but there is no indication of any upward trend (Buchan, 2007).

As in the case of retention, policies to encourage the return of health professionals to the health workforce would need to encompass a mix of financial incentives, career development programmes, and targeted benefits. Some of the main factors that would facilitate attracting nurses back to the clinical workforce, include more flexible hours of work, availability of return-to-work programmes, salary increase, and provision of child care facilities (Zurn et al., 2005). Ireland abolished fees for back-to-practice courses, and nurses and midwives undertaking such courses receive a salary in return for a commitment to rejoin the public health service upon completion of the course. In addition, many of the courses are being delivered on a flexible part-time basis (Department of Health and Children, 2002). Trends over time also suggest that a weak economy encourages nurses to re-enter the health workforce (Aiken and Mullinix, 1987).[11]

3. Adapting skill-mix

Most of the policy attention on using skill-mix[12] changes to improve health-system performance focuses on physicians and nurses. Task shifting between nurse and doctors can improve productivity. However, changing the skill-mix is a challenging task, particularly because of the need to secure the cooperation of the professional groups concerned.

Greece, Korea and Turkey have roughly the same number of doctors and nurses, while in Ireland there are more than five nurses for each doctor. Between these extremes, the ratio of nurses to doctors varies widely across the OECD. Given such variation, it is legitimate to question what should be the appropriate skill-mix between doctors and nurses, and what should be the definition of the respective tasks of these two groups of professionals.

One of the factors which may have affected the growth of density of both doctors and nurses is substitution between them, usually in the form of nurses taking over some of the tasks hitherto performed by doctors. Nurses have been substituted for doctors in a small way in some OECD countries (see for example, Buchan and Calman, 2004; Buchan, 2008). However, as has been shown above, physician numbers have been growing faster than nurse numbers in the majority of OECD countries over the past 15 years. Figure 3.2 suggests that in 17 out of 28 countries for which data are available the ratio of nurses to doctors in 1990 was above that in 2005 (that is, in Figure 3.2, the observation for the country is found to lie below the 45° line). This suggests that technological and economic changes have added more to the demand for doctor-skills than to the demand for nurse skills in these countries over this period.

Figure 3.2. **Change in skill mix between 1990 and 2005 or nearest year available**

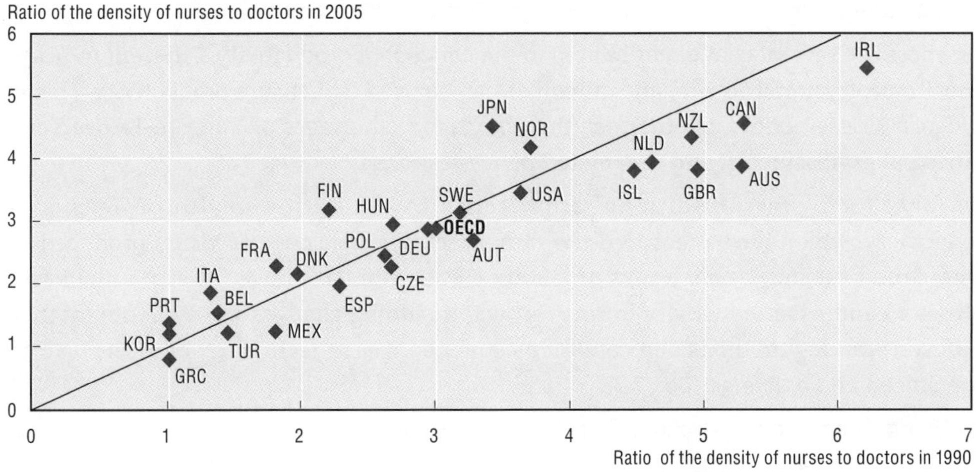

Ratio of the density of nurses to doctors in 2005

Ratio of the density of nurses to doctors in 1990

StatLink ⬛⬛ http://dx.doi.org/10.1787/448324707717

Note: Data refer to practicing doctors and nurses.
Source: OECD Health Data 2007.

Literature reviews of the role of advanced practice nurses (APNs) suggest that nurses can supply care equivalent to that provided by doctors in primary care settings for certain patients. However, the long term benefits or cost from such policies are not yet clearly established (Buchan and Calman, 2004).

Physician assistants are predominantly located in the United States, where this profession was introduced in 1967 (Hooker, 2006). Canada, England, Scotland, Australia, New Zealand and the Netherlands have explored the potential of using physician assistant either to supplement physician services, working under the supervision of a licensed physician, or to deliver tasks usually carried out by doctors. Studies revealed that physician assistants' skills largely overlap with those of primary care physicians, and that they are capable of taking on a high degree of responsibility in other areas of medicine (Hooker, 2006).

While there seems to be a potential for developing new nursing roles and to encourage the use of physician assistants, various factors can hinder this change. Introducing new scope of practice can "blur" frontiers between professions and create tension between, and even within, occupational groups (Kinley et al., 2001). It is not uncommon for professional associations to resist changes in professional boundaries. Institutional factors may also slow down the development of advanced nursing roles. For instance, few countries allow nurses to be reimbursed directly for the new services they provide. Also, given the context of nursing shortages and task shifting, increasing the number of nurses in advanced nursing roles might encourage them to offload tasks to unqualified staff further down the line (Buchan and Calman, 2004).

4. Enhancing health workforce productivity

Improved productivity of physicians and nurses in the workforces can help close upcoming gaps between the demand for and the supply of health professionals. Estimates of productivity are an important adjuster in models of workforce supply and part of increasingly more sophisticated demand-based and trend forecasts of health professionals (Cooper *et al.*, 2002). All other things being equal, improved productivity of human resources would reduce the number of health professionals needed to achieve a given output, or improve throughput delivered with a given level of resources. But, what is the right indicator of productivity, and is it possible to point to an optimal productivity level?

There are several challenges related to the concept of productivity. Different indicators of health professional activity and outcomes can be used to measure productivity. This will influence assessment of whether health systems face shortages or, conversely, oversupply of medical professionals, and the related policy responses.

Take, for a start, traditional approaches to evaluating health professionals' productivity, which have measured the rate of activity (*e.g.,* doctors visits) produced in a given period of time by each unit of labour. OECD countries have implemented several policies to address productivity in this respect, including changes in payments methods, improved working methods and conditions, and changes in technology or in the way care is organised and delivered (Box 3.3).

Using this notion, it appears that the quantum of professionals' supply can be related to productivity levels. Analyses of variation in per capita supply of health professionals across countries, regions, and health-care settings suggest for example that physician productivity may be related to the density of doctors, all other things being equal. Using data from the European Community Household Panel (ECHP) Survey on the annual number of patients' visits to general practitioners (GPs) across the EU15, Figure 3.3 shows a negative, statistically significant, relationship between GP density and the number of visits per doctor. In other words, countries featuring a higher density of doctors appear to have a lower productivity of doctors, as measured by the number of annual visits per doctor.[13] Furthermore, countries with the same number of physicians, such as Switzerland, Denmark and the United Kingdom, display large differences in the number of annual visits, suggesting room for improving productivity.

Supply constraints, if coupled with improved and carefully administered payment systems, have led to enhanced productivity (Docteur and Oxley, 2004). In Finland, sharp cuts in health expenditure in the early 1990s did not seem to have harmed efficiency. On the contrary, they were associated with rises in health centre productivity, measured as activities per unit of real expenditure (OECD, 2005a). In Switzerland, per capita consultations with doctors – at 3.4 in 2002 – were lower than the OECD average of 9.7, while the number of doctors – at 3.6 per 1 000 population – was among the highest in the OECD. Although this may reflect a relatively low revealed demand for health-care services and a relatively good underlying health status of the population, the data also suggest that the same levels of outputs could be achieved with lower resources (OECD, 2005b).

Box 3.3. **Factors and practices influencing professionals' productivity**

Productivity changes over time, as a consequence of external factors and countries' policies. Technological innovation is an important source of change, and offers opportunities for advances in productivity for both nurses and doctors. For example the introduction of day surgery, favoured by technological improvements, led to an increase in the number of surgical procedures that given hospitals and surgery units could perform.

Several workplace and societal changes have a direct impact on productivity. New lifestyle models encourage a better balance between work and private life, leading to shortened working times for health professionals. Earlier retirement by doctors and nurses, as well as increasing part-time working, have a similar effect. In the United Kingdom, while less than 40% of midwives were working part time in 1994, in 2004, more than 60% were working part-time.

Midwives working full and part time, United Kingdom, 1994 and 2004

	Midwives working full time		Midwives working part time		Total number of working midwives
	Number	Percentage	Number	Percentage	
1994	20 889	59.5	14 238	40.5	35 127
2004	12 999	38.6	20 688	61.4	33 687

StatLink http://dx.doi.org/10.1787/448325213477

Source: *Statistical Analysis of the Register*, Nursing and Midwifery Council, August 2005, as reported in Bosanquet *et al* (2006).

Women tend to work fewer hours than their male counterparts during childbearing years and take career breaks, but evidence reviewed by Bloor *et al.* (2006) suggests that women doctors may be less likely to take early retirement. Workforce productivity will show differences across age groups for man and women. Clearly, these factors may vary productivity over a working life time, but will not impact upon productivity per hour worked.

Changes in the way care is delivered and organised, including the use of technologies and the mix of human and non-human resources that provide health services, affect productivity trends. For example, the growing number of elderly patients with chronic illnesses encourages a reorientation of the way care is delivered from cure to care, requiring a different mix of physicians and non-physician health professionals. The successful adoption of new disease management models and of improving care-coordination methods will affect professionals' productivity in these care settings.

Team work can lead to more productive health professionals. Effective teamwork has been recognised as a condition for enhancing clinical outcomes and achieving more with less (see, for example, West *et al.*, 2002; Leggat, 2007). However, further work is required to understand which conditions are best to make teams of health professionals more effective or productive.

Health policies can help in boosting productivity, too. Nurse dissatisfaction and low motivation have led to high turnover and absenteeism. This, in turn, causes reductions in productivity and poor quality of care. Several countries have targeted policies to improve working conditions (including reductions in work intensity) to encourage nurse productivity and reduce turnover (Simoens *et al.*, 2005) (see Section 2.1 in Chapter 2).

> Box 3.3. **Factors and practices influencing professionals' productivity** (cont.)
>
> Payment methods and levels are the most prominent policies to influence productivity of health professionals. Across the OECD, remuneration methods for hospitals, physicians, and other providers have moved away from cost-reimbursement towards activity-based payments that reward productivity (OECD, 2004). Among single payment methods for physicians, fee-for-service – as in the case of office-based physicians in Austria, Belgium, France, Germany, Japan, Korea, Switzerland and the United States (Medicare) – is known for encouraging productivity.
>
> While encouraging productivity, pure activity-related payments may not direct providers to deliver the right quantity and quality of service, and at the right time. For this reason, several countries have introduced blended payment mechanism (which combine a fixed capitation or salary component with a variable fee-for-service element) to promote the provision of cost-effective care. Mechanisms of payment by results (which link payments to the quality of care provided) have also been introduced to reward physicians for the quality of care provided to patients in Australia and in the United Kingdom (Simoens and Hurst, 2006).

Figure 3.3. **The relationship between general practitioner density and the annual number of visits per general practitioners**

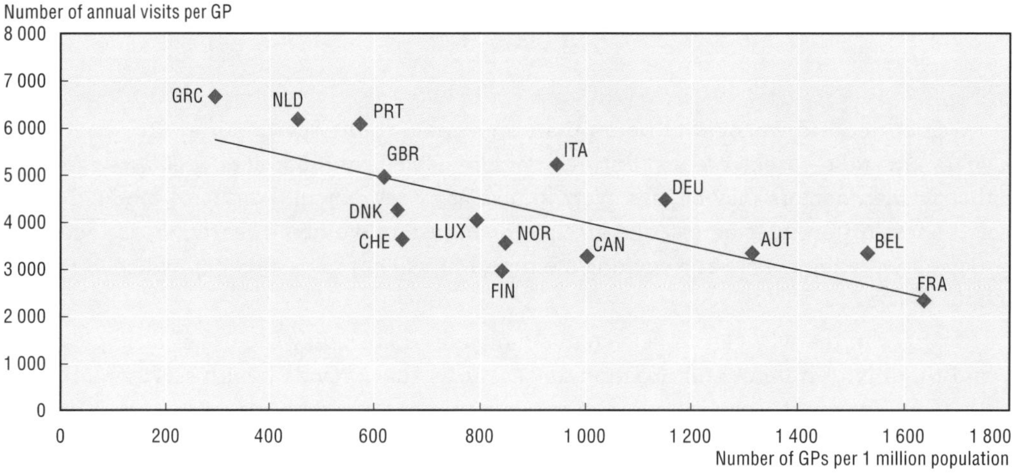

StatLink ᴍᴤᴤ᫁ http://dx.doi.org/10.1787/448332704850

Source: Simoens and Hurst (2006).

That high physician supply is associated with lower productivity has emerged also from analyses of regional and practice-setting variation in per capita supply. For example, work by Wennberg and Cooper (1998) shows that the use of health care services varies dramatically around the United States. These variations are not associated with substantial differences in benefits to the patients. Variation in Medicare spending across US regions – which can be linked to higher-intensity of practice in regions with a higher density of doctors – did not result in better quality of care, or improved health status (Fisher et al., 2003). Similarly, low physician/patient ratios were associated with good health status, as shown by research on large prepaid group practices in the United States (Weiner, 2005).

These studies suggest that, up to a point, low physician's input can come with improved productivity with no harm to patients. They also suggest that improving regional maldistribution of professionals across better-served and least-equipped areas, as well as more equitable distribution of professionals across specialties, may go a long way towards addressing supply gaps.[14] And, thirdly, they point to the fact that more adequate measures of results are needed. The notion of measuring health professionals' services as the output of medical work may need to be questioned.

At present, the output of doctors' work is usually measured by the number of office visits and procedures, a notion similar to the way productivity is calculated in industrial firms. However, physician productivity should be based on improvement of patients' health and responsiveness – the end – rather than physician visits or procedures – the means to the end. Such an approach could be used to incentivise health care workers to provide more adequate care to patients.

Improvements in patient outcomes could be achieved by doing less rather than more. Larger service volumes may in fact be of marginal benefit in terms of improved value for money and patients' health. For example, population based research suggests that above a certain threshold, as use of service increases, quality and health related outcomes do not improve (Weiner, 2007).

On the other hand, a low staff/population ratio can lead to adverse health outcomes if a minimum ratio is not achieved. Very low numbers of doctors can be harmful, as shown for example by analysis on the adverse impact of low supply of neonatal intensive care resources on outcomes (Goodman et al., 2001). Needleman et al. (2002) estimated that higher nurse/patient ratios in the United States were associated with a 3% to 12% reduction in the rates of outcomes potentially sensitive to nursing, such as urinary tract infections and hospital-acquired pneumonia. Another difficulty is in assessing the optimal level of services and accounting for socioeconomic heterogeneity across geographical units (Cooper, 2008).

Unfortunately, the overall evidence is far from being conclusive and it is especially difficult to make inferences about optimal supply levels to maximise people's health. A review of the literature on associations between medical staffing and patient health outcomes concludes that although improvements in patients' outcomes might be possible by expanding doctors' supply, the optimal doctor-to-population ratio is not known (Bloor et al., 2006). Part of the problem lies with difficulties in the measurement of outcomes and quality of care, a developing field.[15] Another difficulty lies with the fact that the notion of the right measure of productivity will depend on broader health-system objectives, which may evolve over time. The desire for more health-system responsiveness, for example, may explain at least part of the apparent association between economic growth and physician numbers. Finally, even assuming the right measures have been developed, mechanisms aligning rewards to the performance of health professionals, are not without risks. Initial results from the United Kingdom's Quality and Outcomes Framework (QOF), for example, suggest that both quality improvement and the payments to practitioners exceeded initial expectations, straining the National Health Service (NHS) coffers (Galvin, 2007; NAO, 2007).

In summary, improvements in health professional productivity have the potential to reduce the rate at which human resources should grow in order to meet future demand expectations. At one extreme, if productivity enhancement occurs at the same rate at which the demand for professional services is growing, then the pressure to build larger stocks of health professionals would disappear. Arguably, other policies such as a better distribution of resources across a country may suffice or at least contribute to meet needs. However, given much uncertainty about the optimal health professionals' ratio to the population, it would not be prudent to count solely on increased productivity to address future needs. Furthermore, questions about the most appropriate way to measure outputs have surfaced. Policy makers should be aware that new concepts based on outcomes and responsiveness may change the way productivity is calculated, and hence the way future needs are assessed.

5. Examples of useful practices

This chapter has discussed the contribution of health workforce policies to make the best use of available workforce and skills. Some examples of useful practices in these areas include the following:

- "Magnet hospitals" are successful in promoting nurse recruitment and retention. They are organisational settings characterised by an emphasis on professional autonomy, decentralised organisational structures, participatory management, and self-governance.

- Admitting more medical students from rural areas to medical schools is a policy with a positive medium and long-term impact on the geographical distribution of doctors as such students are more likely to take up practice in rural areas.

- Providing flexible retirement policies and adapted work for older health workers can improve retention. For example, some countries have enabled staff nearing retirement to move on to part-time work while preserving pension entitlements, or to combine pension and earnings after retirement.

- Attracting back to the health workforce individuals trained as health workers but not active or working in another field, has been adopted successfully in some countries. For example, in Ireland the return of qualified nurses is encouraged by providing back-to-practice courses, and in the United Kingdom improved work-based learning, nursery facilities, and mentoring have had favourable effects.

- Special programmes assist the integration of internationally educated health care workers in countries like Canada, Portugal and the United Kingdom. In the latter, some programmes help refugees who are settled in the country to pass qualification requirements.

- Changing physician/nurse skill-mix, by employing nurses and physician assistants to perform tasks traditionally delivered by physicians, has been shown to be effective in some settings, although less is known about its cost-effectiveness.

- The introduction of ICT systems, better care coordination, disease-management programmes for chronically ill patients, and activity based payments (such as payment by results) can influence the productivity of health professionals.

Further work is necessary however to assess the opportunity cost of different policies and refine productivity measurement, thereby helping policy makers in trading-off between different options.

Notes

1. For instance, the national turnover rate for Registered Nurses in the United States was 15.5% in 2003 (COMON, 2006).

2. Turnover expresses the percentage of a defined labour force that is lost each year through retirement, death, international migration or occupational changes.

3. The NEXT-Study is investigating the reasons, circumstances and consequences surrounding premature departure from the nursing profession in several European countries (Belgium, Finland, France, Germany, Great Britain, Italy, the Netherlands, Poland, Sweden, and in Slovakia).

4. For example, more than 40% of nurses working in hospitals report dissatisfaction with their job in the United States, Canada, England, Scotland, and Germany (Aiken et al., 2001).

5. In Sweden, health care has even been reported to be the sector with the highest risk of violence (Chappel and Di Martino, 1999).

6. For example, in France, 2 900 doctors left the profession in 2004 while 3 500 graduated (Cash and Ulmann, 2008). In Italy, a country with a lower nurse density than the OECD average, around 12 500 nurses retired each year between 1997-2002, whereas the yearly number of new graduates was 5 700 during that period (Camerino, 2006).

7. In Germany, only 6.2% of qualified nurses were 55 years old and over in 2002, compared to 11.1% of female workers as a whole (Hasselhorn et al., 2006).

8. In Australia, for example, the nursing retirement rate will be significantly higher between 2006 and 2026, than it was between 1986 and 2001. Between 2006 and 2026 Australia is projected to lose almost 60% of the current nursing workforce to retirement (Schofield, 2007).

9. Or around 6 000 individuals who purchased an Annual Practicing Certificate.

10. Or 488 000 registered nurses.

11. In the United States, for example, inactive nurses returning to work along with nurse immigration accounted for a substantial share of the growth of the employed nurse workforce over the period 2000-2003 following a period of decline in nurse graduations (Buerhaus et al., 2003)

12. Skill mix is a relatively broad term which can refer to the mix of staff in the workforce or the demarcation of roles and activities among different categories of staff.

13. Unfortunately, it is not possible to control for visit duration.

14. As has been shown in various studies on the United States and the United Kingdom. However, doctors tend not to settle where care is most needed. See, for example, Goodman et al. (2001) and Gravelle and Sutton (2001).

15. The OECD is pursuing a project to develop a set of health care quality indicators based on comparable data across 23 countries (www.oecd.org/health/hcqi). This will help to fill existing gaps in the measurement of health care quality across countries.

ISBN 978-92-64-05043-3
The Looming Crisis in the Health Workforce:
How Can OECD Countries Respond?
© OECD 2008

Chapter 4

International Mobility of Health Workers: Interdependency and Ethical Challenges

Growing international mobility of health professionals needs to be better monitored. Intra-OECD movements of health professionals account for an important share of health worker immigration to OECD countries, inducing cross-OECD interdependency in the management of health human resources. Ultimately there is a risk of exporting shortages within or beyond the OECD area, including to the poorest nations. Migration from countries which train to supply the world market cannot be a complete solution if all receiving countries turn to a limited number of origin countries which also have to respond to an increasing domestic demand in the near future. The global health workforce shortage, which goes far beyond the migration issue, calls for a shared responsibility between sending and destination countries. Origin countries must strength their health systems, improve domestic working conditions and encourage better management of their workforce. Host countries, on the other hand, must be aware of the impact of their policies on the health systems of impoverished nations. However, good practice for an ethical management of international recruitment raise several implementation and conceptual challenges, making the concept of shared responsibility difficult to operationalise. There is a need for greater international sharing of knowledge about useful examples with a view to their assessment and if appropriate, replication.

There is increased cross-country interdependence, both in terms of imbalances in the distribution of health human resources and in terms of management of health human resources. Specific conditions and policies in the health sector of a given country can affect directly or indirectly the health systems of other countries. Meanwhile, structural shortage of health personnel in low-income countries, no matter what their causes, could weaken health systems, and thus, in the long run, jeopardise global public health. International mobility of doctors and nurses can either ease or accentuate these challenges, depending on their scope, characteristics (*e.g.* origin-destination, occupations, duration) and their "side" effects (*e.g.* technological transfers, investment in human capital abroad, remittances).

This means that countries should not consider the management of health human resources in isolation. Rather they need to take into account the influence that other countries' policies will have on their own health system, and vice-versa, as well as potential global impacts. This chapter identifies and discusses the main interactions across OECD countries, and between OECD and other countries (Section 1). It then draws attention to possible policies for better sharing the benefits of the international mobility of health professionals and to ethical dimensions of international recruitment (Section 2).

1. Cross-national impact of the international recruitment of health workers

The growing international mobility of health professionals within the OECD, which can be depicted through a cascade model, calls for better monitoring and coordination tools across OECD countries. This would be especially critical if several OECD countries were to experience health workforce shortages simultaneously, as reliance on a selected number of abundant-supply origin countries might not be a sustainable solution.

1.1. *Migration within the OECD: a cascade model*

Intra-OECD movements of health professionals represent an important share of immigrant health workers (see Figure 4.1). This is notably the case for nurses in Nordic countries, Ireland, Switzerland and New Zealand, and for doctors in Norway, Switzerland, Belgium or Austria. This finding, observed for stocks, also applies to recent trends in flows.

International mobility of health professionals within the OECD usually reflects general migration patterns, which are determined by language and geographic proximity, cultural and historical ties and bilateral migration policies. Such flows may generate interconnected migration channels, for example nurses move from the Slovak to the Czech Republic and from there to Germany, but there are also movements from Germany to the United Kingdom and finally from the United Kingdom to the United States. In other cases, movements occur mainly within a limited group of OECD countries, for example across Australia, New Zealand and the United Kingdom in the case of doctors. Finally, some intra-OECD flows are mainly bilateral. Migration between Mexico or Canada and the United States, or between France (in the case of nurses) or Germany (in the case of doctors) and Switzerland are an illustration.

Figure 4.1. **Share of foreign-born doctors and nurses originating from within the OECD area, *circa* 2000**

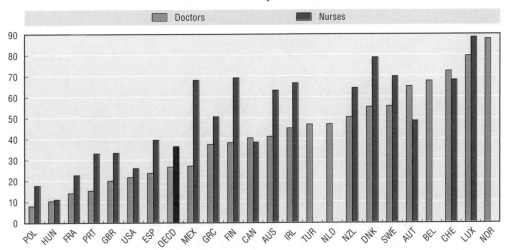

StatLink ᴍᴸ☞ http://dx.doi.org/10.1787/448342231253

Note: OECD weighted average.

Source: OECD (2007a), *International Migration Outlook*, Paris.

Overall, a cascading migration model can well illustrate the interactions between OECD countries (see Figure 4.2 for nurses; the representation for doctors would be similar). Some countries appear as net receivers of health professionals *vis-à-vis* most other OECD countries, while others are predominantly net senders.

The United States is the only net-receiver country, *i.e.*, it receives more health-professional immigrants than it sends emigrants to all other OECD country.[1] As a result, the United States is shown at the bottom of the cascading model. Canada, Australia, and Switzerland – also net receivers of health professionals from most OECD countries – are similarly positioned at the lower end of the cascade. In the case of Canada, however, the large nurse emigration to the United States generates a negative net intra-OECD migration (–6 000).

Intra-OECD movement of health personnel is likely to continue, if not increase, in the near future. Several factors lie behind this trend, for example: the persistence of historical rights; the development of a free or facilitated mobility area, as the case of the European Union (Box 4.1);[2] differences in levels of health professionals' remuneration (Figure 4.3); few or unpromising work prospects in the origin countries;[3] arrangements to facilitate the recognition of foreign OECD qualifications; and the increasing intra-OECD mobility of other categories of migrants (*e.g.* foreign students, highly-skilled professionals and researchers, or intra-company transferees).

Due to cross-OECD interdependency, structural unbalances between the supply of, and the demand for, doctors or nurses, as well as specific policy changes, may impact the management of health human resources in other countries. New Zealand, a country with large immigration and emigration of doctors and nurses from and to other OECD countries, provides an interesting example in this regard. Changes in Australian and/or UK policies, respectively the main destination and source country, can have sizeable impacts on availability of human resources in New Zealand (Zurn and Dumont, 2008). Similarly, changes in the demand for immigrant doctors or nurses in the United Kingdom will directly affect migration from countries with which wage differentials are the largest, such as Poland, the Baltic states, Bulgaria and Romania. Because of its size and attractiveness, anticipated

Figure 4.2. **Intra-OECD migration of nurses: a cascade-type pattern**

Net stocks, *circa* 2000

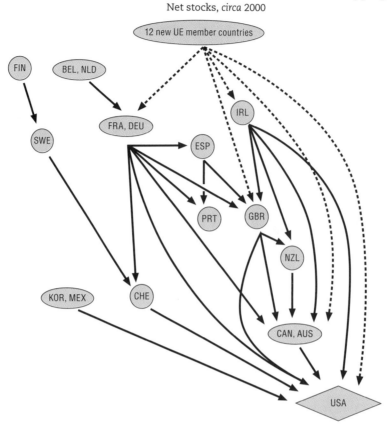

Note: Arrows represent a positive difference between the stocks of nurses in origin and receiving countries. Not all possible downward arrows are represented (for instance Finland has a net deficit with Sweden but also with Switzerland and the United States), but there would be no ascending arrows (for instance at the time of the population census Ireland has only a net gain with regards to 12 new EU member countries and the United States was the only country to have a net gain *vis-à-vis* all other OECD countries).

Source: OECD (2007a), *International Migration Outlook*, Paris.

Box 4.1. **The consequence of recent EU enlargement on health worker migration flows**

Although only partial evidence is available to date, the May 2004 and December 2007 European Union enlargements encouraged movements from "new" to "old" EU members. Between July 2004 and December 2007, the Worker Registration Scheme in the United Kingdom registered 730 hospital doctors, 370 dental practitioners, more than 1 000 nurses (including 365 dental nurses) and 485 nursing auxiliaries and assistants as originating from the new member states (Home Office, 2008). In Ireland, the employment of EU8 nationals in the health sector doubled between September 2004 and 2005, from 700 to about 1 300 persons (Doyle *et al.*, 2006). Data from origin countries confirm these trends. In Estonia, 4.4% of health professionals (61% of which were physicians) had applied for a leave certificate by April 2006. In Latvia, more than 200 doctors expressed their intention to migrate in 2005. Poland issued more than 5 000 leave certificates to doctors (4.3% of the active workforce) and around 2800 to nurses (1.2% of the active workforce) between May 2004 and June 2006 (Kaczmarczyk, 2006). A systematic analysis of the trends and consequences of these movements – including for Romania and Bulgaria that have recently joined the European Union and face even greater salary disparities with the EU25 group (Wiskow, 2006) – would be welcome.

Figure 4.3. **Remuneration of GPs, selected OECD countries, 2004 or closest year available**

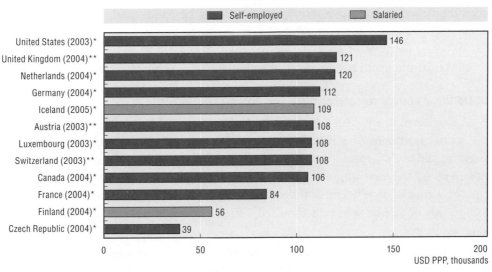

A. In USD PPP

| | Self-employed | Salaried |

United States (2003)*	146
United Kingdom (2004)**	121
Netherlands (2004)*	120
Germany (2004)*	112
Iceland (2005)*	109
Austria (2003)**	108
Luxembourg (2003)*	108
Switzerland (2003)**	108
Canada (2004)*	106
France (2004)*	84
Finland (2004)*	56
Czech Republic (2004)*	39

USD PPP, thousands

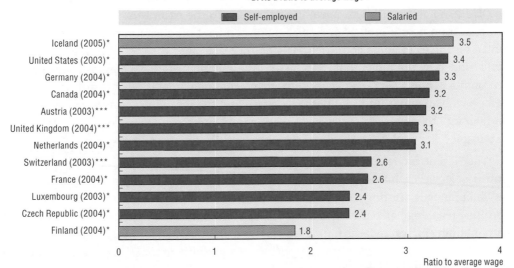

B. As a ratio to average wage

| | Self-employed | Salaried |

Iceland (2005)*	3.5
United States (2003)*	3.4
Germany (2004)*	3.3
Canada (2004)*	3.2
Austria (2003)***	3.2
United Kingdom (2004)***	3.1
Netherlands (2004)*	3.1
Switzerland (2003)***	2.6
France (2004)*	2.6
Luxembourg (2003)*	2.4
Czech Republic (2004)*	2.4
Finland (2004)*	1.8

Ratio to average wage

StatLink http://dx.doi.org/10.1787/448345750816

* Indicates that the average remuneration refers only to physicians practicing full time.
** Refers to the average remuneration for all physicians including those working part-time (thereby resulting in an underestimation). In Austria, Switzerland and the United States, data refer to all physicians (both salaried and self employed) but since most GPs are not salaried in these countries, they are presented as referring to self-employed physicians. For the United Kingdom, data refer to Great Britain.
*** Refers to the average remuneration for all physicians including those working part-time.
Source: OECD Health Data 2007 and for the United States, Community Tracking Study Physician Survey, 2004-05.

shortages in the United States, particularly for nurses, could have significant consequences for other OECD countries. Mexico, Canada, the United Kingdom and Germany, traditional source countries for health professionals in the United States, could be the most concerned.

Intra-OECD movements of highly-skilled workers, including health professionals, need to be monitored, if not anticipated, to avoid exporting shortages across OECD countries, and ultimately outside the OECD area. Cross-national interdependency requires better co-ordination mechanisms, including monitoring procedures, both within and outside the OECD area. These could be considered as part of bilateral or multilateral frameworks, and could involve mechanisms ranging from extended information exchanges to joint planning exercises. Better international monitoring of medical workforce flows, including migration movements by country of origin and training, graduation rates and movements out of the workforce (notably retirements) would help develop better pictures of overall health-worker flows, improve capacity to assess the impact of migration, and hence design adequate policies solutions.

1.2. Do large source countries offer the "cornu copiae"?[4]

As discussed in Chapter 1, many OECD countries could simultaneously face health professional shortages. If migration were to play a significant role in addressing these shortages, one could expect a net inflow from the rest of the world to the OECD area. This scenario raises the question of whether migration from certain high-supply and low-cost countries would be an efficient solution for filling expected gaps in many OECD countries. Setting aside equity issues for a moment,[5] such a strategy does not promise to offer a lasting solution.

As OECD standards for health professionals are high, international recruitment could increasingly concentrate on a limited number of source countries. India and the Philippines, for example, already supply most of the foreign-trained doctors and nurses to the OECD,[6] notably to English-speaking countries. To the extent that these major source countries train health professionals for export, emigration does not decrease the pool of human resources in home countries.[7] Furthermore, because the cost of training is at least partly funded by the individual in India and the Philippines, the social loss borne by the community in home countries is minimised. International migration of health workers can then provide an opportunity for both the origin and the receiving country, as a well as for the migrants themselves. However, to what extent are these examples transferable and sustainable?

The Filipino model for "exporting nursing schools" can probably be developed in other countries. However, further expansion in the Philippines is probably not possible. In fact, the Philippines is starting to experience difficulties in controlling quality of training, in recruiting teaching personnel who have access to attractive job opportunities abroad, and in maintaining high standards for patient-focused practice. In addition, Filipino doctors are retraining as nurses to get better opportunities for foreign work, so that the country effectively waste money training them.

Training doctors for export is also an option, but it would be especially complicated because the cost of training is high and success in the study less systematic. Supplying the world with graduate doctors paying the full cost of training in private institutions would require a large middle income class able to support expensive studies for their siblings.[8] Developing training capacity in medical schools and guaranteeing quality standards would also pose challenges.[9] Brazil, India and China are probably the most suitable candidates for such developments. "Medical cities" are already mushrooming in India and most of them include private medical schools.[10] However, the internal demand is also increasing rapidly and India still has a very low density of doctors (0.6 per thousand population). In the Caribbean countries, medical schools offer places for US citizens, at lower cost and additional to US places.

Reliance on recruiting from such export countries, clearly raises risks. OECD countries may compete for recruitment of health professionals from a limited number of origin countries. The latter could, as a result, face difficulties in expanding their training capacity to cope with rapidly increasing internal and external demand for doctors and nurses. Despite their size, China, India and Brazil might not represent an unlimited source of health professionals.

2. International recruitment of health workers: ethical concerns

International migration of health professionals generates controversy over the relative advantages and risks for home countries. Concerns have been expressed that the costs for sending countries might outweigh the benefits, especially in the case of migration from poor countries – nearly three-quarters of foreign-born doctors and two-thirds of foreign-born nurses originate from non-OECD countries. These are legitimate concerns, if one considers that health systems in developing countries are often fragile and undersized in relation to public health challenges.[11] However, to be useful for policy makers, the debate should be framed from a broader perspective. This is what this section attempts to do. After discussing briefly how workforce migration compares with the size of health professional shortages in source countries, this section reviews the impact of migration on human capital formation and health systems' capacity in such countries, and certain underpinning factors. It then reviews strategies and practices that have been proposed or implemented to address concerns about fairness arising from international migration of health professionals.

2.1. The size of the brain drain in relation to global shortages

OECD analysis suggests that international migration is not the main cause of the developing world's health human resources crisis, although it contributes to exacerbate the acuteness of the problems in some countries (Dumont and Zurn, 2007).

Health workforce shortages experienced by developing countries are far greater than the number of immigrant health workers to the OECD. The World Health Organization's estimates of regional health professional shortages largely outstrip the number of foreign-born health professionals who have emigrated to OECD countries. This means that even considering an unrealistic hypothetical scenario where migration from developing countries were to stop, these countries would still face up to considerable health human resource gaps.

Africa is a compelling case. The magnitude of the workforce crisis in the continent is worrying. According to the *World Health Report* (2006), of the 57 countries facing critical physician shortages worldwide, 36 are found in Africa. Put another way, over three quarters of the 47 African countries face shortages. According to WHO estimates, a 140% increase in the current stock of health professionals would be required to meet demand in Africa. Yet, African-born health professionals working in the OECD area account for only 12% of the WHO's estimated need for doctors and nurses in the region (Dumont and Zurn, 2007). South-East Asia is another example. Six of the eleven countries in this region are plagued by critical shortages that, according to WHO estimates, could be met by doubling existing stocks of health professionals in the region. Yet, professionals born in the South-East Asian countries and working in OECD countries make up only 9% of those estimated needs.[12]

2.2. Is health professional migration a threat or an opportunity for source countries?

Several features of health professional migration influence how beneficial or detrimental it can be for sending countries, namely: the size of the estimated needs for health professionals in home countries; the role of remittances; the duration of migration; and the split of training costs between origin and destination countries.

The size of shortages in source countries

Migration of health professionals from large developing countries will not have the same impact on origin countries as migration from small or impoverished countries facing significant health-professional shortages (Dumont and Zurn, 2007).

The outflow of health professionals from large origin countries such as India, Russia or China – albeit large in absolute terms – remains low compared to their total workforce.[13] Some countries with high expatriation rates manage to maintain relatively high density of health professionals at home. This is the case notably for countries which train for export, such as the Philippines and some Caribbean states for nurses.

This contrasts with the case of smaller countries, where emigration decreases the ability to deliver quality care to the population and to provide quality training to remaining health professionals. Working conditions may then deteriorate for doctors and nurses who stay, adding to their incentives to leave. Out-migration of health professionals, expressed as a percentage of health professionals who left the country, are especially high in Caribbean and African countries, notably Portuguese and French-speaking countries, but also Sierra Leone, Tanzania, Liberia and to a lesser extent Malawi (see Maps 4.1 and 4.2).

Remittances mitigate the impact of the emigration of health workers only to a limited extent

Amongst the potential positive effects, remittances are often quoted as contributing to improving the health status of those left behind. Evidence is in fact quite mixed. A few studies using micro data tend to confirm a positive, although small and not always robust, role of remittances on the health outcomes of children.[14] In contrast, macro level analyses have found that emigration of women with tertiary education, many of whom will be working in the health sector, impacts negatively upon infant and under-five mortality rates in origin countries. This may suggest that the negative health impact deriving from the absence of qualified mothers is not offset by the positive role of remittances (Dumont et al., 2007).

Considering international migration of health professionals specifically, it is unlikely that the negative effects due to the departure of health personnel could be compensated, at the macro level, by remittances. The latter remain private money, which is often used for consumption and only in small part for saving and investment.[15] It does not contribute to health systems development, nor compensate for the economic disruption caused by high rates of emigration. Furthermore, because health professional migrants are highly-skilled workers who are more likely to come from wealthier families, remittances are unlikely to reach the poorest and those most at risk in terms of health (e.g. only 6% of poor Mexican households receive remittances).

Previous arguments do not necessarily exclude positive linkages between remittances and the health sector, although these are neither automatic nor direct. The tres por uno programme in Mexico, which supports community investment in local infrastructure, provides an interesting example in this regard.[16]

Map 4.1. **Expatriation rates for doctors by country of origin**

Percentages, circa 2000

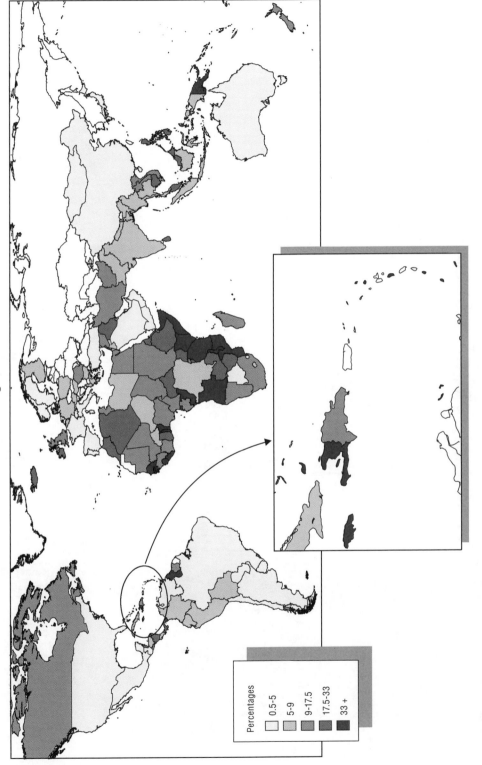

Percentages

- 0.5-5
- 5-9
- 9-17.5
- 17.5-33
- 33 +

Source: Dumont and Zurn (2007).

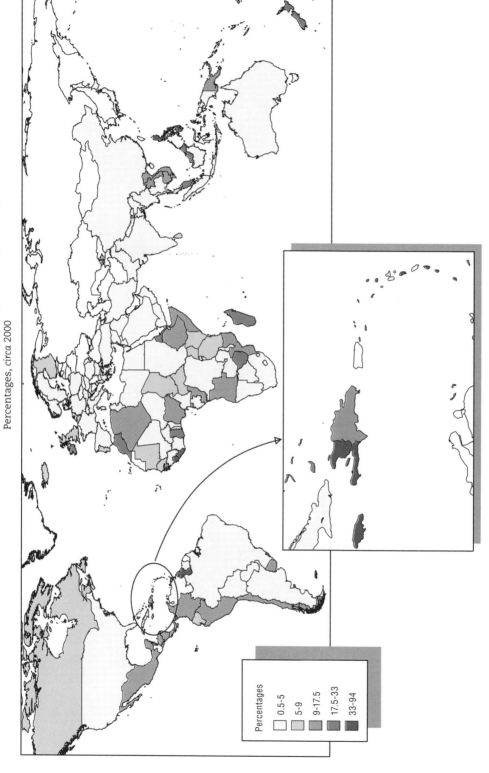

Map 4.2. **Expatriation rates for nurses by country of origin**
Percentages, circa 2000

Percentages

- 0.5-5
- 5-9
- 9-17.5
- 17.5-33
- 33-94

Source: Dumont and Zurn (2007).

Duration of overseas stays is critical to the potential impact on origin countries

The duration of stay of migrant health workers is another important feature that can influence how beneficial is migration to origin countries. Temporary migration may enable doctors and nurses to gain professional experience abroad, acquire exposure to new medical techniques, and upgrade their skills (assuming that they are not over qualified in their job and that their new skills respond to the most urgent health care needs in their home country). Permanent migration, on the other hand, represents a permanent loss of human capital for the home country and leads to added cost for recruiting replacements, which is unlikely to be compensated by financial flows back to the country.

The *ex ante* distinction between temporary and permanent migration is however difficult to make in practice, notably because most OECD countries have made it easier to change from temporary to permanent status. Also, initial migration intentions may change over time as the health workers spend time and integrate in the receiving country.[17] The employers themselves do not always encourage high turnover of migrants, as this increases the fixed costs for the recruitment and the integration of foreign workers. Finally, the transferability of the skills acquired abroad depends on the working and reintegration conditions in the home country. Some evidence suggests that health professionals returning to their origin countries may not have their new qualification recognised and are therefore effectively downgraded.[18]

Migrants will consider returning permanently to their origin country when the conditions which motivated their departure are no longer met. Surveys exploring health workers' reasons to migrate identify issues such as a safer environment, and better living conditions, facilities, career opportunities and remuneration (Awases *et al.*, 2005; Vujicic *et al.*, 2004). The possibility to raise children in an international and high-quality school system also plays a key role. These "social reasons" for emigration are not confined however to health professionals.

Return is not a necessary condition for health workers to contribute to the health system of their origin country. Beside remittances, diasporas play a role particularly when successful migrants visit their countries of origin for teaching activities and highly-specialised medical interventions. Some OECD countries actively encourage these efforts by mobilising highly-skilled migrants to support economic development in their country of origin. This is for instance the case of France, in the context of "co-development" agreements with French-speaking African countries.

Developing countries also benefit, albeit on a small scale from paid and voluntary work by health professionals of OECD origin (Laleman *et al.*, 2007). OECD countries should support these initiatives, for example by adapting the workload of those involved and by recognising the value of the professional activities undertaken in the context of voluntary technical assistance.

Who pays for what?

A last element in a cost and benefit evaluation of health worker migration is training and education costs, and their financing. The loss sustained by home countries will be high if foreign professionals have received training at home, and even more so if training was publicly subsidised.

According to OECD analysis, comparisons of health professional migration reveal lower percentages of foreign-trained professionals than foreign-born ones in the health workforces in destination countries (Dumont and Zurn, 2007). The difference can be explained, at least partly, by the fact that some of the foreign-born professionals receive training in the destination countries, either because they moved (often as children) with their families or as a result of internationalisation of medical education. Evidence suggests that the role of foreign medical students has been growing recently. Some of them, especially at postgraduate levels, are however migrant health professionals whose home country qualifications are not fully recognised.

2.3. Policy responses

Addressing the global health workforce crisis and critical shortages in developing countries will require policy responses beyond migration policies in home and host countries. As already observed, shortages outweigh international migration by a large margin in many low-income countries, and, therefore, policy solutions must address the many factors underpinning such crisis. Yet, receiving countries should be alert and sensitive to the impact that migration flows have on origin countries. This is especially true for impoverished nations that are facing critical shortages of health human resources. Widening international imbalances in the distribution of health human resources could also encourage the dissemination of disease and, in the long run, jeopardize global public health.

The role of originating countries

Governments and policy makers in countries that are facing workforce shortages have a role to play in searching for policy responses to reduce outflows and to strengthen health systems in source countries. Unless public health systems in origin countries are supported by improving working conditions, alternative policies and practices at both national and international level will be insufficient.

Assessment of the relative importance of in and outflows, their determinants, and their impact on the health system, is clearly an important first step. Migration of those already in health sector employment to other countries may be one main source of health worker outflows, but is not always the main or only one. Workers may simply leave the health profession in search for better paid or more motivating jobs in the country in question or may be unable to find employment in their profession in the first place. Understanding what is happening and why will help designing actions to counterbalance movements out of the health workforce (Buchan, 2007).

The internal distribution of the health workforce is a great challenge for low-income countries, maybe even more than international migration. Imbalances between the rural and the urban areas or between the private and the public sectors raise major public-health concerns. The World Health Report (WHO, 2006) estimates that, on average, while 55% of the population lives in urban areas, these areas concentrate 75% of the doctors and 60% of the nurses. The imbalances in some developing countries can be even higher.[19]

There is an urgent need for action to improve domestic working and living conditions, including educational opportunities and security, along with domestic policies to train, attract and retain doctors and nurses in the source country. Although solutions can be hard to identify considering the strong financial constraints faced by many countries, some have successfully improved health-worker retention using a combination of monetary and non-monetary incentives.

Malawi provides such an example. It has been possible to improve retention and reduce unfilled vacancies, with major financial support from the UK Department for International Development (DFID), over a six-year period. The measures include increasing salary (+52%), increasing staffing (+7%), doubling the training intake of nurses and tripling that of doctors, developing hardship incentive package in 137 underserved rural areas (30% of facilities). Similar schemes were put in place with the support of Dutch aid in Zambia (Tyson, 2007). Other countries, such as Ghana, have attempted to provide doctors with an advantageous car hire-purchase scheme and preferential access to housing loans for all health personnel. However, they had to face resentment among those in other professions not entitled to participate in the schemes.

To recover the cost of socially funded education, some developing countries, such as Ghana and South Africa, have implemented schemes whereby the government sustains medical and nursing training cost and requires, in exchange, that graduates work for public health services for a few years. Alternatively, medical graduates must buy back their bond before they can work overseas. These bonding schemes, however, have been often ineffective and have provided incentives to leave in several countries. Implementation has been complicated, among other things, by difficulties in monitoring compliance. Destination countries can help to make these arrangements more effective by ensuring that they do not recruit workers who have not fulfilled their obligations at home.

Broader issues related to health workforce management and policies in developing countries have been dealt with extensively by the *World Health Report* (WHO, 2006). International experience offers an opportunity to share positive and negative experience and learn from useful practices across both developed and developing countries.

The role of host countries in ethical management of international recruitment

Some OECD counties have adopted or considered specific policies to mitigate the negative impact and reinforce the benefits associated with the migration of health personnel, as described below. These provide interesting examples to be shared and eventually generalised or scaled up. Nevertheless, such mechanisms generate theoretical and practical challenges. It is difficult to co-ordinate such policies across different public-sector players and governmental levels and almost impossible to bar direct recruitment by the private sector. In particular, it has proved difficult to address concerns about specific impoverished source countries without discriminating against particular professional groups or individuals from these countries. While there is no internationally recognised "right to migrate", individuals' freedom to move and to seek professional and personal development opportunities outside their country of origin should be acknowledged.

Codes of conduct and agreements. Codes of practice and intergovernmental agreements have been proposed to foster ethical recruitment of health professionals. Such codes seek to identify countries from which recruitment may be less harmful and to suggest ethical forms of recruitment from poor countries. Examples of voluntary, non-legally binding instruments have been developed since 1999. Their diffusion has however been limited and their effectiveness questioned.

At a national level, the United Kingdom has taken the lead in establishing *codes of ethical conduct* for international recruitment of healthcare professionals. The Department of Health published a Code of practice (2001, revised in 2004) setting guiding principles for ethical recruitment and employment of migrant healthcare professionals (Department of

Health, 2004). The code seeks to prevent targeted recruitment from developing countries experiencing healthcare staff shortages. All health organisations, including the independent sector, can sign up to the principles contained within the code.

The most cited example of multilateral codes is the Commonwealth's International Code of Practice for the International Recruitment of Health Workers. The code, produced in 2003, sets principles to guide governments in international recruitment of health workers (Commonwealth Secretariat, 2003). The European Federation of Nurses has similarly produced principles of ethical recruitment, while the European Union is currently trying to develop a similar declaration. Other initiatives have included the so-called "Melbourne Manifesto"[20] and the "London Manifesto",[21] both of which include specific guidelines and principles for fair recruitment (Labonte et al., 2006). Finally, the 57th World Health Assembly in 2004 urged member states to address health worker migration issues, and, in particular, requested the WHO secretariat to propose an international Code of Practice on migration. The responses to this initiative are beyond the scope of this report.

Bilateral agreements can be used to improve the management of international mobility of health workers, notably if they include clauses whereby a recipient country agrees to: underwrite the costs of training additional staff; and/or to recruit staff for a fixed period only, prior to their returning to the source country; and/or to recruit surplus staff in source countries (Buchan, 2007). For example, the United Kingdom has developed bilateral agreements or memoranda of understanding for the recruitment of health workers with a number of countries, including South Africa, India, the Philippines, Spain, China and Indonesia. Japan also has an agreement with the Philippines for nurses, which includes an important training component. Some Italian regions also have innovative bilateral agreements for nurses with a number of Romanian regions.

The effectiveness of ethical codes and intergovernmental agreements will depend on: the content (principles envisaged, practical details), the coverage (countries and employers involved), and the compliance (mechanisms utilised, effectiveness) of these arrangements. Martineau and Willets (2006) review existing instruments, highlighting limits to their effectiveness due to the lack of: support systems, incentives and sanctions, and monitoring systems. Mcintosh et al. (2007) underline the many practical difficulties facing Canada in implementing ethical recruitment of internationally educated health professionals, notably in balancing individual rights, meeting international equity concerns, and in defining the concept of active recruitment.

Regulating the role of recruitment agencies

With the increasing demand for health care workers in OECD countries, many recruitment agencies have emerged as intermediaries between international health care workers and employers in OECD countries. To a certain extent, these recruitment agencies stimulate the migration of health workers.

Although there is a lack of information concerning the operations of these recruitment agencies, a report published by the ILO has indicated that two thirds of the 400 international migrant nurses in London were recruited by agencies in the United Kingdom (ILO, 2006). Some of these nurses reported being underpaid and hired for low-skilled jobs, particularly in the long-term care sector where significant shortages exist. In some instances, the agency has acted directly as the employer providing short-term placement (Connell and Stilwell, 2006). Additionally, some international recruitment agencies, national health services and private healthcare institutions have conducted active recruitment campaigns overseas (Dobson and Salt, 2007).

Concerns over the recruitment conditions of health professionals hired through agencies, as well as the effect on origin countries experiencing shortages of health workers, have prompted regulation of recruitment agencies in some OECD countries. Five countries (Australia, Italy, Netherlands, Poland and the United Kingdom) have regulated the use of recruitment agencies for health professionals (Dumont and Zurn, 2007). To address the issue of recruiting health workers from developing countries, the United Kingdom was the first to implement an ethical code of practice which restricts the recruitment of health workers from over 150 developing countries. Also, the UK National Health Service (NHS) recommends only using recruitment agencies that comply with the Code of Practice for both domestic and international recruitment, and it lists these approved agencies.

Better sharing of training cost. Some source countries advocate a compensation mechanism which involves a transfer of money (or other form of compensation) from the destination country to the origin country, proportional to migration flows of doctors and nurses. The argument goes as follows: social externalities associated to health justify public investment in training of health workers, but workers' migration constitutes an implicit loss of such training cost and a subsidy to the destination country, which should be repaid, or at least compensated for. In the 1970s and 1980s, Bhagwati suggested that migrants could pay a special tax to finance education systems in developing countries (Bhagwati, 1976; Bhagwati and Partington, 1976).

This approach poses several conceptual and practical difficulties. For example, financial reparation should be evaluated taking into account: i) employment opportunities in the home country (ex-ante); ii) the duration of stay in the receiving country (ex-post); as well as iii) the share of the cost of training that was funded by the migrant, the receiving country and the country of origin or of training. Furthermore, this approach poses ethical question for those who flee their home country for humanitarian reasons because of conflict or persecution.

These difficulties explain why, although much discussed, to date compensations have not been implemented systematically. The Commonwealth Code of International Recruitment of Health Workers and the 2007 Pacific Code of Practice are – to our knowledge – the only international agreements that mention a compensation clause. The Commonwealth Code does not specify, however, mechanisms or principles to implement it. Among OECD countries only New Zealand has signed this code.

Part of the problem with compensation is the link between migration and monetary transfers. Some people have suggested that developed countries could contribute to a voluntary educational reinvestment fund to expand training in the developing world (Joint Learning Initiative, 2004). This would be a way to compensate origin countries for their loss of investment in training and education. A UK report assessing policy options to reduce health professional migration also suggested a compensation equivalent to the salaried value of health workers employed in receiving countries (Mensah et al., 2005). This option, however, has been criticised and dismissed (Labonte et al., 2006).

Welcoming foreign medical students. Scholarships and grants for students from developing countries to study medicine in destination countries help to build skills which would otherwise have been difficult to acquire in home countries.

The return to investment for the origin country is conditioned by the return of the professional for a certain number of years following graduation. Several origin countries providing their students with publicly-financed scholarships to study medicine abroad require health professionals to return home to practice, or repay back the loans and grants they received. Issuing non-extendable visas to foreign students from poorer countries is sometimes mentioned as an option for destination countries.

Norway, for example, offers scholarship to about 1 100 students from developing countries, including eastern and central Asian countries. The scholarship is offered under the same conditions as Norwegian students, as a mixed loan and grant. If the student returns home, the loan is converted into a grant. The J1 *exchange visitor skill* visa in the United States stipulates that students must return for two years to their former country of permanent residence before applying to another US visa.[22] Under the Medical Training Initiative, the United Kingdom recently introduced a specific, non-renewable training and work-experience visa for third country nationals who receive a training sponsorship by the Royal Colleges and other organisations within the medical field. Changes in the 2006 immigration law in France make it easier for foreign students to shift status, although they also stipulate that, ultimately, the student is required to return to the origin country.

Imposing return clauses has however proved to be difficult, if not inefficient. People may prefer to leave for another receiving country, rather than return home. They may gain the right to remain in the country, through marriage for instance. Such policies also raise ethical trade-offs between the right of individual migrants to better himself/herself economically by moving to destination countries and the concern about the loss for the health systems of exporting nations. Applying restrictions on health worker migrants from underserved origin countries would involve rights discrimination on the grounds of place of origin and therefore be illegal under anti-discrimination law in many countries.

Even without specific return clauses, there is certainly a potential for welcoming more foreign medical and nursing students in some OECD countries. Some of them will return home after completing their studies, which will benefit origin countries especially when these latter did not support training costs, while those staying on will add to the workforce of the residence country.

Foreign aid and technical assistance. By strengthening the health systems of developing countries, international development initiatives could help to mitigate the push factors that make health professionals leave their own countries and that might jeopardise the achievement of the Millennium Development Goals.

OECD countries have long-term commitments through their aid agencies to improve living standards in developing countries. Efforts to achieve better health outcomes for the poor are an integral component of donors' poverty reduction strategies (OECD, 2003). By providing technical support and mobilising adequate financial resources, international aid plays an important role in building health human resource capacity. Donors can encourage the introduction of health workforce policies in Poverty Reduction Strategies drafted by developing countries. They can also support investments in training and education systems in the countries exporting skilled staff. For example, the UK Department for

International Development supports programmes to strengthen health systems in developing countries, including investment in training, and incentives and hardship allowances for workers working in rural areas (DFID, 2007).

Donors can also help to develop networks in source countries that draw on the experience of migrant professionals working in more developed nations and, in this way, foster knowledge transfer across the health systems of origin and destination countries. The United States Agency for International Development supported the Nursing Quality Improvement Program, to associate US hospitals accredited for nursing excellence as part of the Magnet Recognition Program with hospitals in Russia and Armenia. Such strategies help to reduce the "push" factors associated with the lack of professional roles and opportunities for nurses in low income countries (Aiken and Cheung, 2008).

Donor countries' are placing emphasis on ensuring policy coherence across aid and other national policies, and this is clearly the case when it comes to health workforce and international migration issues. For example, the European Union adopted in 2005 a Strategy for Action with strong focus on addressing the lack of health professionals in developing countries and avoiding brain drain, especially with respect to Africa.[23] Since the EU Tripoli conference on migration and development in November 2006, and with the launch, at the Lisbon Summit in December 2007, of the EU-Africa Partnership on Migration, Mobility and Employment, European and African heads of states have agreed to policies to reduce brain drain from origin countries. Health has also been identified as a "tracer" sector for monitoring the impact of aid policies in the light of the September 2008 High-Level Forum on Aid Effectiveness in Accra (Ghana). The issue of migration of health professionals has thus become an integral element of multi-party efforts to ensure overall policy coherence for development.

Although smaller in scale, migration of health workers from developed to poor countries, including volunteers, can offer a noteworthy contribution to developing countries, especially if it is well coordinated with the receiving countries (Laleman *et al.*, 2007). Such individuals can help to train health care workers in the receiving country, and motivate them not to leave. They often fill vacant jobs and can help in addressing emergencies, as, for example, has happened under the auspices of several non-profit organisations.

Notes

1. The difference between OECD health professionals in the United States and US-born health professionals in other OECD countries is about 79 000 for nurses and of 44 000 for doctors.

2. In addition, the European Union, the North American Free Trade Agreement, or the Trans-Tasman Agreement between New Zealand and Australia.

3. For example, Italy suffers from a noteworthy brain drain for the highly skilled, including doctors. This is partly due to the high density of medical doctors in the population, partly to the dismal employment outlook, leading many doctors, to migrate, notably to other EU countries (Chaloff, 2008). A similar situation concerns some of the OECD eastern European countries.

4. *Cornu copiae*: a symbol or emblem of abundance.

5. See Section 2 of Chapter 4 for a discussion of ethical issues and possible solutions.

6. According to the 2000 censuses data, about 15% of the immigrant doctors in the OECD have originated from India and the same percentage of nurses were born in the Philippines. This pattern is maintained in recent flows.

7. Some authors even argue that in such a case, increasing migration opportunities would have a positive impact on the disposable stock of highly-skilled workers in the source country (*e.g.* Stark, 2004; Beine *et al.*, 2007). If this is true under very strict hypotheses (perfect market for credit, non selection process, low emigration rate), it certainly does not apply to most of the smaller or least advanced countries, especially in the case of health professionals where most of the training is at least partly publicly funded.

8. For example, in India, training costs for full-fee paying students are generally about USD 40 000 for the duration of the training. Cost of living and other costs should be added on top.

9. The issue of quality could be addressed by developing partnerships through international medical schools. The campus created by Monash University in Malaysia for example offers equivalence to Australian standards (it graduates about 100 persons per year; undergraduate training for international students cost approximately USD 35 000 for five years full-time course; post graduate training costs about USD 22 000 for four years).

10. The private sector accounted for 45% of the medical colleges in India in 2004 (10 685 places), and grew by 900% between 1970 and 2004. This compares to 36% for public institutions over the same period, and a growth of only 20% (13 320 places in 2004) (Mahal and Mohanan, 2006).

11. " The African Region for instance suffers more than 24% of the global burden of disease but has access to only 3% of health workers and less than 1% of the world's financial resources – even with loans and grants from abroad " (WHO, 2006).

12. As for the Americas and Western Pacific, foreign-born professionals working in OECD countries outstrip estimated local needs, however the picture here is partially blurred by the fact that a large share of immigrants have been trained in OECD countries or originate from a limited number of large countries.

13. The expatriation rate of Chinese doctors is about 1% while that of India reaches 8%.

14. The World Bank (2006) shows that, in the case of Guatemala, children from households that report receiving remittances tend to exhibit higher health outcomes than those from non-recipients households with similar demographic and socio-economic characteristics, after controlling for pre-migration income. Most results however do not hold for Nicaragua. Moreover, Adams (2006) finds no impact of international remittances on the marginal budget share on health expenditure in Guatemala. In the case of rural Mexico, Hildebrandt and McKenzie (2005) show that children in migrant households (not households receiving remittances) have lower infant mortality and higher birth weights.

15. For this reason, comparing expected remittances sent by health professionals to the training cost supported by the public authorities would not be sound.

16. In 1993, the state government of Zacatecas, Mexico, introduced the programme "Dos por Uno" (Two for One), in which both the federal and state governments match one dollar for each dollar that home town associations contribute to development projects in Zacatecas. By 1999, the programme had expanded to include local governments and became "Tres por Uno" (Three for One), encompassing not just the state of Zacatecas but also other Mexican states such as Guanajuato, Jalisco, and Michoacan. In 2005, Mexican home town associations raised about USD 20 million for development projects throughout Mexico, which was matched by USD 60 million in Mexican federal, state, and local government contributions (*www.migrationinformation.org/USfocus/display.cfm?ID=579*).

17. Unfortunately data on return migration for doctors and nurses are not available.

18. This was the case for nurses in South Africa for instance (Dumont and Meyer, 2004).

19. Two-thirds of the doctors in Ghana, for example, are to be found in the two largest towns of Accra and Kumasi (Nyonator and Dovlo, 2005).

20. A code of practice for the international recruitment of health care professionals adopted by delegates to the World Organization of National Colleges, Academies and Academic Associations of General Practitioners/Family Physicians (WONCA) meeting in Melbourne, Australia on 3 May 2002.

21. An agreement resulting from an international conference on the global health workforce organised on 14 April 2005 by the British Medical Association in association with the Commonwealth. Participants included the American Medical Association, the American Nurses Association, the Commonwealth Medical Association, the Commonwealth Nurses Federation, Health Canada, the Medical Council of Canada, the Royal College of Nursing and the South African Medical Association.

22. Except if eligible to J1 waiver programme.

23. EU Strategy for Action on the Crisis in Human Resources for Health in Developing Countries.

ISBN 978-92-64-05043-3
The Looming Crisis in the Health Workforce:
How Can OECD Countries Respond?
© OECD 2008

Chapter 5

Conclusion: The Way Forward

It has been reported that many OECD countries are facing potential shortages of health workers over the next 20 years. The demand for health workers is expected to increase because of rising incomes, continuing technological change in medicine and the ageing of OECD populations. The stock of health workers will fall, as the "baby boom" generation is beginning to reach retirement age. Individual OECD countries will face four main options to close the prospective gap between the demand for and supply of health workers over the next two decades. These are: to train more staff at home; to improve the retention and delay the retirement of existing OECD health workers; to raise productivity of existing health workers; and to recruit health workers internationally from other OECD countries or from outside the OECD area.

At the international level, there is growing awareness of the implications of migration for resource-poor countries with low-starting health professional densities. The ability to recruit from countries with high health professional densities may not be sustained in the long-term if many countries start recruiting from a limited number of origin countries. These dilemmas are influencing policy discussions and the search for alternatives at both national and international level. They call for better tracking and monitoring of the effects of different policy mixes adopted by countries. Importantly, the role and impact of health professionals' migration should be looked at within the context of broad workforce policies.

Individual OECD countries will face four main options to close the prospective gap between the demand for and supply of health workers over the next two decades. These are: to train more staff at home; to improve the retention and delay the retirement of existing OECD health workers; to raise productivity of existing health workers; and to recruit health workers internationally from other OECD countries or from outside the OECD area.

1. Additional training

Many OECD countries have already increased their training rates for doctors and nurses. Countries could try to fill the projected remaining gaps between demand and supply that have been estimated in some countries by training even more health workers. The rapid rate at which some countries have increased their training programmes in recent years suggests that training capacity might be expandable even further.

However, it can take five years to fully train nurses and more than ten years to fully train doctors. Filling additional posts – especially "hard-to-fill" posts – may require an increase in relative remuneration, putting additional pressure on the wage bill. Choosing the training option could conflict with the objective of containment of public expenditure. In many countries, the training costs currently fall partly or mainly on the public sector. In such countries, it may be helpful to consider shifting more of the cost of training towards the private sector by imposing fees and financing them through loans.

Nevertheless, education and training remains the most important and direct policy tool for building the health workforce. Current efforts devoted by OECD countries in this context contribute to addressing the global health workforce crisis.

2. Encouraging retention and delaying retirement

There may be scope for improving the retention of OECD health workers and delaying retirement. In the case of nurses, there is evidence from several OECD countries that nurse turnover and dissatisfaction is high. More investment in initiatives such as the US "Magnet Recognition Program", which approves institutions which show excellence in the organisation of nursing care, could help to improve retention of nurses as well as raise nurse productivity. Turning to retirement, rising expectation of life in OECD countries introduces the possibility that working lives may be extended. Many OECD countries have already begun to raise official retirement ages or to make retirement more flexible.

3. Raising productivity

So long as certain trends in the health workforce continue, such as reducing hours of work, increasing part time working, and, in the case of the medical profession, increasing specialisation and feminisation, there will tend to be a rise in headcounts in relation to full time equivalent workers. This prospect should add to the stimulus for a search for higher productivity.

OECD countries may be able to raise the productivity of their health workers in a number of ways in the next couple of decades. These could include: labour-saving technological changes such as accelerating the introduction of IT systems in health care; further improving skill-mix in the health workforce, particularly by the further expansion of roles for physician assistants and nurse practitioners; and improving the relationship between pay and performance.

4. Recruiting internationally

Like education, but without the long delays, international recruitment has a direct impact on the stock of health workers. For this reason, immigration could appear as an attractive option when there are unanticipated surges in demand. There are potential gains from migration for both receiving countries and migrants. It may be possible to recruit rapidly experienced staff. Migrants are often ready to accept "hard-to-fill" posts in the host country. They may help to maintain the continuity of services in the host country and they will significantly contribute to adapting health care services to the needs of increasingly culturally diverse OECD societies. Meanwhile, migrants themselves are likely to benefit if the host country can offer posts with better pay and conditions than are available to them in the sending country.

If there are countries with surplus and others with shortages, international migration of health professional can provide efficiency gains both at the global and the individual levels. Furthermore, if the cost of training is at least partly funded by the individual, the social loss to home countries is minimised. In this context, international migration of health workers could provide an opportunity for both the origin and the receiving country, as a well as for the migrants themselves. However, there are doubts about the sustainability of this option in the case of developing countries as the demand for health care will also increase with economic development.

When there is no identifiable surplus country, international migration would still generate potential gains for the migrants themselves and the receiving country facing recruitment difficulties. However, if training is publicly funded, the opportunity for migration is a potential source of a free rider-type problem, which gives rise at the level to a loss of efficiency, with less effort devoted to education and training in receiving countries. However, restricting the right to emigrate gives rise to equity concerns: individuals should have the right to seek opportunities internationally. Nevertheless, OECD countries share with origin countries concerns about the risks of global shortages and brain drain, particularly when this affects small states with low starting density of health professionals.

Reducing reliance on migration by addressing structural imbalances in OECD countries, improving health human resource planning, as well as improving workforce distribution and deployment certainly go hand in hand with confronting some of the ethical concerns about international recruitment of health human resources from poorer source countries. Aid and international co-operation programmes in OECD countries are devoting growing attention to this issue in the context of their commitment towards health for all. There is also ongoing discussion in both home and destination countries about ethical recruitment, although its potential to influence migration flows and the extent of international recruitment is probably limited. Unless public health systems in origin countries are strengthened, by improving working conditions, thus ensuring better retention within the profession and the country, practices which attempt to block outflows are unlikely to succeed.

To the extent that immigration and emigration of health workers continues, there is no guarantee that all these policies will *add up* across countries. Shortages, and indeed surpluses, of health workers can be exported from one country to others. This is why, given the uncertainty about migration flows, there is a strong case for better international communication about health workforce policy and planning. In addition, continued effort to improve the availability and comparability of data on international migration of health workers is desirable. This would not only help in diagnosing potential imbalances between demand and supply in the global market for health workers. It would also improve the prospects for international co-ordination.

ISBN 978-92-64-05043-3
The Looming Crisis in the Health Workforce:
How Can OECD Countries Respond?
© OECD 2008

References

AACN – American Association of College of Nursing (2005), "With Enrollment Rising for the 5thConsecutive Year, US Nursing Schools Turn Away 30,000 Qualified Applicants", available at *www.aacn.nche.edu/Media/NewsReleases/2005/enrl05.htm*.

AAMC – Association of American Medical Colleges (2006), *AAMC Statement on the Physician Workforce*.

Adams, R.H. (2006), "International Remittances and the Household: Analysis and Review of Global Evidence", *Journal of African Economies*, Vol. 15, Supplement No. 2, pp. 396-425.

AHA – American Hospital Association (2007), *AHA Survey of Hospital Leaders*.

Aiken, L.H. and R. Cheung (2008), "Health Workforce and International Migration: A Case Study on Nurses in the United States", OECD Health Working Paper, forthcoming, OECD, Paris.

Aiken, L.H. and c.f. Mullinix (1987), "The Nurse Shortage: Myth or Reality?", *New England Journal of Medicine*, Vol. 317, No. 10, pp. 641-646.

Aiken, L.H. *et al.* (2001), "Nurses' Reports on Hospital Care in Five Countries", *Health Affairs*, May/June, pp. 43-52.

Allan, H. and J. Larsen (2003), "We Need Respect: Experiences of Internationally Recruited Nurses in the UK", Presented to the Royal College of Nursing.

Antonazzo, E. *et al.* (2003), "The Labour Market for Nursing: A Review of the Labour Supply Literature", *Health Economics*, Vol. 12, pp. 465-478.

Awases, M. *et al.* (2005), "Migration of Health Professionals in Six Countries: A Synthesis Report", WHO Regional Office for Africa.

Bach, S. (2003), "International Migration of Health Workers: Labour and Social Issues", Working Paper No. 209, ILO, Geneva.

Barer, M.L. and G.L. Stoddart (1991), "Toward Integrated Medical Resource Policies for Canada", prepared for the Federal/Provincial/Territorial Conference of Deputy Ministers of Health.

Beine, M., F. Docquier and H. Rapoport (2008), "Brain Drain and Human Capital Formation in Developing Countries: Winners and Losers", *The Economic Journal*, Vol. 118, No. 528, pp. 631-652, April.

Bessiere, S. *et al.* (2004), "La démographie médicale à l'horizon 2025", *Études et Résultats*, No. 352, DREES, Paris, November.

Bhagwati, J.N. (eds.) (1976), *The Brain Drain and Taxation – Theory and Empirical Analysis*, Amsterdam, North-Holland, pp. xi-292.

Bhagwati, J.N. and M. Partington (eds.) (1976), *Taxing the Brain Drain – A Proposal*, Amsterdam, North-Holland, pp. xiii-222.

Bloor, K. *et al.* (2006), "Do We Need More Ddoctors?", *Journal of the Royal Society of Medicine*, Vol. 99, pp. 281-287, June.

Bosanquet, N. *et al.* (2006), "Staffing and Human Resources in the NHS – Facing up the Reform Agenda", Reform Thinktank, London.

Bourgueil, Y., J. Mousques and A. Tajahmadi (2006), "Improving the Geographical Distribution of Health Professionals: What the Literature Tell Us", *Questions d'Économie de la Santé*, No. 116, IRDES, Paris.

Brush, B., J. Sochalski and A. Berger (2004), "Imported Care: Recruiting Foreign Nurses to the US Health Care Facilities", *Health Affairs*, Vol. 23, No. 3, pp. 78-87.

Buchan, J. (2004), "Here to Stay? International Nurses in the UK", Paper Commissioned by the Royal College of Nursing, available at *www.rcn.org.uk/publications/pdf/heretostay-irns.pdf*.

Buchan, J. (2007), "Health Worker Migration in Europe: Assessing the Policy Options", *Eurohealth*, Vol. 13, No. 1, pp. 6-8.

Buchan, J. (2008), "Health Workforce and International Migration: A Case Study on the United Kingdom", OECD Health Working Paper, forthcoming, OECD, Paris.

Buchan, J. and L. Calman (2004), "Skill Mix and Policy Change in the Health Workforce: Nurses in Advanced Roles", OECD Health Working Paper, No. 17, OECD, Paris.

Buchan, J., R. Jobanpura and P. Gough (2005), "Should I Stay or Should I Go?", *Nursing Standard,* Vol. 19, No. 36, pp. 14-16.

Buerhaus, P.I., D.O. Staiger and D.I. Auerbach (2003), "Is the Current Shortage of Hospital Nurses Ending?", *Health Affairs,* Vol. 22, No. 6, pp. 191-198.

Butler, C. and J. Eversley (2005), *More than You Think: Refugee Doctors in London, their Numbers and Success in Getting Jobs*, Refugee Doctor Programme Evaluation Network, London.

Camerino, D. (2006), "Factors Influencing Turnover among Italian Qualified Nurses", Presentation at the 28th International Congress on Occupational Health, Milan, 11-16 June 2006, available at *www.next.uni-wuppertal.de/download/conway2006b.pdf*.

Camerino, D. *et al.* (2006), "Low-perceived Work Ability, Ageing and Intention to Leave Nursing: A Comparison among Ten European Countries", *Journal of Advanced Nursing*, Vol. 56, No. 5, pp. 542-552, December.

Cash, R. and P. Ulmann (2008), "Migration des professionnels de santé : le cas de la France", OECD Health Working Paper, forthcoming, OECD, Paris.

Chaloff, J. (2008), "Mismatches in the Formal Sector, Expansion of the Informal Sector: Immigration of Health Professionals to Italy", OECD Health Working Paper, forthcoming, OECD, Paris.

Chan, B. (2002), *From Perceived Surplus to Perceived Shortage: What Happened to Canada's Physician Workforce in the 1990s?*, Canadian Institute for Health Information.

Chappell, D. and V. Di Martino (1999), "Violence at Work", *Asian-Pacific Newsletter on Occupational Health and Safety,* Vol. 6, No. 1.

Chiha, Y.A. and C.R. Link (2003), "The Shortage of Registered Nurses and Some New Estimates of the Effects of Wages on Registered Nurses Labour Supply: A Look at the Past and a Preview of the 21st Century", *Health Policy*, Vol. 64, pp. 349-375.

COGME – Council of Graduate Medical Education (2005), *Physician Workforce Policy Guidelines for the United States*, Sixteenth Report, 2000-2010.

Commonwealth Secretariat (2003), *The Commonwealth Code of Practice for the International Recruitment of Health Workers*, London.

COMON – Coalition of Michigan Organizations of Nursing (2006), "The Nursing Agenda for Michigan: 2005-2010: Actions to Advert a Crisis", COMON, available at *www.michigancenterfornursing.org/mimages/NAText06.pdf*.

Connell, J. and B. Stilwell (2006), "Recruiting Agencies in the Global Health Care Chain", in C. Kuptsch (ed.), *Merchant of Labour*, ILO, Geneva.

Cooper, R. (2008), "The US Physician Workforce: Where Do We Stand?", OECD Health Working Paper, forthcoming, OECD, Paris.

Cooper, R. *et al.* (2002), "Demographic Trends Signal an Impending Physician Shortage", *Health Affairs,* Vol. 21, No. 1, pp. 140-154.

Dalphond, D. *et al.* (2000), "Violence against Emergency Nurses", *Journal of Emergency Nursing*, Vol. 26, pp. 105-109.

Dauphinee, D. (2006), "The Circle Game: Understanding Physician Migration Patterns within Canada", *Academic Medicine*, Vol. 81, Supplement No. 12, pp. 49-54.

Department of Health (2004), "Code of Practice for the International Recruitment of Healthcare Professionals", London.

Department of Health and Children (2002), "The Nursing and Midwifery Resource: Final Report of the Steering Group: Towards Workforce Planning", Dublin.

DFID – Department for International Development (2007), *Moving out of Poverty – Making Migration Work Better for Poor People*, London.

Dobson, J. and J. Salt (2007), "Foreign recruitment in Health and Social Care: Recent Experience Reviewed", *International Journal of Migration, Health and Social Leave,* Vol. 2, No. 3/4, pp. 41-57.

Docteur, E. and H. Oxley (2004), "Health-care Systems: Lessons from the Reform Experience", OECD Health Working Paper, No. 9, OECD, Paris.

Doyle, N., G. Hughes and E. Wadensjo (2006), *Freedom of Movement for Workers from Central and Eastern Europe,* Swedish Institute for European Policy Studies (SIEPS), Stockholm.

Dumont, J.C. and J.B. Meyer (2004), "The International Mobility of Health Professionals: An Evaluation and Analysis Based on the Case of South Africa", *Trends in International Migration,* SOPEMI Edition 2003, OECD, Paris.

Dumont, J.C. and P. Zurn (2007), "Immigrant Health Workers in OECD Countries in the Broader Context of Highly-skilled Migration", *International Migration Outlook,* Part III, OECD, Paris, pp. 162-228.

Dumont, J.C. and P. Zurn (2008), "Health Workforce and International Migration: A Case Study on Canada", OECD Health Working Paper, forthcoming, OECD, Paris.

Dumont, J.C., J.P. Martin and G. Spielvogel (2007), "Women on the Move: The Neglected Gender Dimension of the Brain Drain", IZA Discussion Paper, No. 2920, Bonn.

Ebihara, S. (2007), "More Doctors Needed Before Boosting Clinical Research in Japan", *The Lancet,* Vol. 369, No. 9579, p. 2076.

Expert Panel on Health Professional Human Resources (2001), "Shaping Ontario's Physician Workforce", Ontario Minister of Health and Long-Term Care.

Farrell, G.A. (1999), "Aggression in Clinical Settings: Nurses' Views – A Follow-up Study", *Journal of Advanced Nursing,* Vol. 29, pp. 532-541.

Fisher, E.S. *et al.* (2003), "The Implications of Regional Variations in Medicare Spending", Part 1: The Content, Quality and Accessibility of Care, *Annuals of Internal Medicines,* Feb. 18, Vol. 138, No. 4, pp. 273-287.

Galvin, R. (2007), "Pay-for-Performance: Too Much of A Good Thing? A Conversation with Martin Roland", *Heath Affairs,* Vol. 25, pp. w412-w419.

Goodman, D. (2004), "Do We Need More Physicians? The Answer Is to be Found in a Reexamination of Physician Productivity", *Health Affairs,* Web Exclusive, W4-67.

Goodman, D.C. *et al.* (2001), "Are Neonatal Intensive Care Resources Located According to Need? Regional Variation in Neonatologists, Beds, and Low Birth Weight Newborns", *Pediatrics,* Vol. 108, No. 2, pp. 426-431.

Gravelle, H. and M. Sutton (2001), "Inequality in the Geographical Distribution of GPs in England and Wales 1974-1995", *Journal of Health Services Research and Policy,* Vol. 6, No. 1, pp. 6-13.

Gupta, N. *et al.* (2003), "Assessing Human Resources for Health: What Can Be Learned from Labour Force Surveys?", *Human Resources for Health,* Vol. 1, No. 5, available at *www.pubmedcentral.nih.gov/picrender.fcgi?artid=179883&blobtype=pdf.*

Hasselhorn, H.M., B.H. Muller and G.P. Tackenber (2005), *NEXT Scientific Report,* University of Wuppertal, Wuppertal.

Hasselhorn, H.M., G.P. Tackenberg and A. Buescher (2006), "Work and Health of Nurses in Europe: Results from the NEXT-Study", University of Wuppertal, Wuppertal.

Hawthorne, L. (2006), *Labour Market Outcomes for Migrant Professionals: Canada and Australia Compared,* Citizenship and Immigration Canada, Ottawa.

Hawthorne, L., G. Hawthorne and B. Crotty (2006), *The Registration and Training Status of Overseas Trained Doctors in Australia,* Faculty of Medicine, Dentistry and Health Sciences, The University of Melbourne, Melbourne.

Hildebrandt, N. and D. McKenzie (2005), "The Effects of Migration on Child Health in Mexico", Policy Research Working Paper Series, No. 3573, The World Bank and University of Nevada, Department of Resource Economics, Reno.

Home Office (2008), *Accession Monitoring Report,* May 2004-December 2007.

Hooker, S. (2006), "Physician Assistants and Nurse Practitioners: The United States Experience", *The Medical Journal of Australia,* Vol. 185, No. 1, pp. 4-7.

House of Commons (2007), "Health Committee: Workforce Planning: Fourth Report of Session 2006-7", The Stationary Office, London.

HRSA – Health Resources and Services Administration (2004), *What is Behind HRSA's Projected Supply, Demand and Shortage of Registered Nurses?*, HRSA, Rockville, September.

Igushi, Y. (2006), *Growing Mismatches of Health Professionals in Japan*, Kwansei Gakuin University.

ILO – International Labour Organisation (2006), *Merchant of Labour*, C. Kuptsch (ed.), ILO, Geneva.

IMF – International Monetary Fund (2007), "World Economic Outlook", *Spillovers and Cycles in the Global Economy*, Chapter 5, IMF, Washington, DC.

Janus, K. et al. (2007), "German Physicians on Strike – Shedding Light on the Roots of Physician Dissatisfaction", *Health Policy*, Vol. 82, pp. 357-365.

Joint Learning Initiative (2004), *Human Resources for Health – Overcoming the Crisis*, Cambridge.

Joyce, C., et al. (2007), "Riding the Wave: Current and Emerging Trends in Graduates from Australian University Medical Schools", *Medical Journal of Australia*, Vol. 186, pp. 309-312.

Kaczmarczyk, P. (2006), "Highly Skilled Migration from Poland and Other OECD Countries – Myths and Reality", Reports and Analyses , Vol. 17/06, Center for International Relations, Warsaw.

Kangasniemia, M., L.A. Winters and S. Commander (2007), "Is the Medical Brain Drain Beneficial? Evidence from Overseas Doctors in the UK", *Social Science and Medicine*, Vol. 65, pp. 915-923.

Kinley, H.C. et al. (2001), "Extended Scope of Nursing Practice: A Multicentre Randomised Controlled Trial of Appropriately Trained Nurses and Preregistration House Officers in Pre-operative Assessment in Elective General Surgery", Health Technology Assessment, London.

Kolars, J. (2001), "Forecasting Physician Supply and Demand", *Medical Education*, Vol. 35, No. 5, pp. 424-425.

LaBonte, R., C. Packer and N. Klassen (2006), "Managing Health Professional Migration from Sub-Saharan Africa to Canada: A Stakeholder Inquiry into Policy Options", *Human Resources for Health*, Vol. 4, No. 22.

Laleman, G., G. Kegels, B. Marchal, D. Van der Roost, I. Bogaert and W Van Damme (2007), "The Contribution of International Health Volunteers to the Health Workforce in Sub-Saharan Africa", *Human Resources for Health*, Vol. 5, No. 19.

Leggat, S.G. (2007), "Effective Healthcare Teams Require Effective Team Members: Defining Teamwork Competencies", *BMC Health Service Research*, Vol. 7, No. 17, accessible at *www.pubmedcentral.nih.gov/articlerender.fcgi?artid=1800844#B3*.

Lennon, B. (2005), "Medical Workforce Expansion in Australia – Commitment and Capacity", 9th Medical Workforce Collaborative Conference.

Mahal, A. and M. Mohanan (2006), "Medical Education in India: Implications for Quality and Access to Care", *Journal of Educational Planning and Administration*, Vol. 20, No. 4, pp. 173-184.

Mahoney, R. et al. (2004), "Shortage Specialties: Changes in Career Intentions from Medical Student to Newly Qualified Doctor", *Medical Teacher*, Vol. 26, No. 7, pp. 650-654, November.

Martin, J. (2007), "Editorial – The Medical Brain Drain: Myths and Realities", *Trends in International Migration*, SOPEMI Edition 2007, OECD, Paris.

Martineau, T. and A. Willetts (2006), "The Health Workforce: Managing the Crisis Ethical International Recruitment of Health Professionals: Will Codes of Practice Protect Developing Country Health Systems?", *Health Policy*, Vol. 75.

Maybud, S. and C. Wiskow (2006), "Care Trade: The International Brokering of Health Care Professionals", in C. Kuptsch (ed.), *Merchant of labour*, ILO, Geneva.

Maynard, A. (2006), "Medical Workforce Planning: Some Forecasting Challenges", *The Australian Economic Review*, Vol. 39, No. 3, pp. 323-329.

Mcintosh, T., R. Torgeson and N. Klassen (2007), "The Ethical Recruitment of Internationally Educated Health Professionals: Lessons from Abroad and Options for Canada", CPRN Research Report H/11, Health Network.

Mensah, K., M. MacKintish and L. Henry (2005), *The "Skills Drain" of Health Professionals from the Developing World: A Framework for Policy Formulation*, Medact, London.

Minore, B. et al. (2005), "The Effects of Nursing Turnover on Continuity of Care in Isolated First Nation Communities", *Canadian Journal of Nursing Research*, Vol. 37, No. 1, pp. 86-100.

NAO – National Audit Office (2007), *Pay Modernisation: A New Contract for NHS Consultants in England*, NAO, 19 April.

Needleman, J. *et al.* (2002), "Nurse-Staffing Levels and the Quality of Care in Hospitals", *The New England Journal of Medicine*, Vol. 346, No. 22, pp. 1715-1722.

Nursing Council New Zealand (2006), *Workforce Statistics Update*, Nursing Council New Zealand, Wellington.

Nyonator, F. and D. Dovlo (2005), "The Health of the Nation and the Brain Drain in the Health Sector", in T. Manuh (ed.), *At Home in the World? International Migration and Development in Contemporary Ghana and West Africa*, Accra, Sub-Saharan Publishers, p. 229.

NZHIS – New Zealand Health Information Service (2002), *New Zealand Nurses and Midwives 2000*, NZHIS, New Zealand.

O'Brien-Pallas, L. *et al.* (2006), "The Impact of Nurse Turnover on Patient, Nurse, and System Outcomes: A Pilot Study and Focus for a Multicenter International Study", *Policy, Politics and Nursing Practice*, Vol. 7, pp. 169-179.

OECD (2003), *Poverty and Health – DAC Guidelines and Reference Series*, OECD, Paris.

OECD (2004), *Towards High-Performing Health Systems*, OECD, Paris.

OECD (2005a), *OECD Review of Health Systems – Finland*, OECD, Paris.

OECD (2005b), *OECD Review of Health Systems – Switzerland*, OECD, Paris.

OECD (2006a), "The Supply of Physician Services in OECD countries", OECD Health Working Paper, No. 21, OECD, Paris.

OECD (2006b), "Projecting OECD Health and Long-term Care Expenditures: What Are the Main Drivers?", Economics Department Working Paper, No. 477, OECD, Paris.

OECD (2007a), *International Migration Outlook*, OECD, Paris.

OECD (2007b), *Health at a Glance*, OECD, Paris.

OECD (2007c), *Regions at a Glance*, OECD, Paris.

O'Connell, B. *et al.* (2000), "Nurses' Perceptions of the Nature and Frequency of Aggression in General Ward Settings and High Dependency Areas", *Journal of Clinical Nursing*, Vol. 9, pp. 602-610.

Omeri, A. (2006), "Workplace Practice with Mental Health Implications Impacts on Recruitment and Retention of Overseas Nurse in the Context of Nursing Shortage", *Contemporary Nurse*, Vol. 21, No. 1.

Ordre National des Médecins (2006), *Étude de la Problématique des PADHUE*, Paper adopted during the 28 April 2006 session of National Council of the Medical Order, Dr Xavier Deau, Président de la Section Formation et Compétences Médicales, available at *www.web.ordre.medecin.fr/rapport/padhue2006.pdf*.

Ormanczyk, M.E., C.M. Naftalin, A.C. Kydd and R.F. Cooper (2002), "Will More Women Choose a Surgical Career when Working Hours are Reduced?", *Bulletin of The Royal College of Surgeons of England*, Vol. 84, No. 8, pp. 264-268, September.

Paragona (2006), "Polish Doctors to Work in the Royal Danish Armed Forces", Press Release, 5 May.

Peterson, C.A. (2001), "Nursing Shortage: Not a Simple Problem – No Easy Answers", *Online Journal of Issues in Nursing*, Vol. 6, No. 1.

Reitz, J.G. (2001), "Immigrant Skill Utilization in the Canadian Labour Market: Implications of Human Capital Research", *Journal of International Migration and Integration*, Vol. 2, pp. 347-378.

Schofield, J. (2007), "Replacing the Projected Retiring Baby Boomer Nursing Cohort 2001-2026", *BMC Health Service Research* 7:87; available at *www.pubmedcentral.nih.gov/picrender.fcgi?artid=1906767&blobtype=pdf*.

Secretary of State for Health (2000), *The NHS Plan: A Plan for Investment. A Plan for Reform*, HMSO, London.

Shamian, J. *et al.* (2003), "Nurse Absenteeism, Stress and Workplace Injury: What Are the Contributing Factors and What Can/Should Be Done about It?", *International Journal of Sociology and Social Policy*, Vol. 23, pp. 81-103.

Shield, M. (2004), "Addressing Nurse Shortages: What Can Policy Makers Learn from the Econometric Evidence on Nurse Labour Supply?", *The Economic Journal*, Vol. 114, pp. F464-F498, November.

Simoens, S. and J. Hurst (2006), "The Supply of Physician Services in OECD Countries", OECD Health Working Paper, No. 21, OECD, Paris.

Simoens, S., M. Villeneuve and J. Hurst (2005), "Tackling Nurse Shortages in OECD Countries", OECD Health Working Paper, No. 19, OECD, Paris.

Stark, O. (2004), "Rethinking the Brain Drain", *World Development*, Vol. 32, No. 1, pp. 15-22.

Tyson, S. (2007), "Human Resources for Health – Ignorance-based Policy Trends", DFID, Presentation at Sussex University, "Human Resources for Health and Migration: Mobility, Training and the Global Supply of Health Workers", 14-16 May.

USDHHS – US Department of Health and Human Services (2006), *Registered Nurse Population: Findings from the March 2004 National Sample Survey of Registered Nurses*, Washington, DC.

Von Zweck, C. and P. Burnett (2006), "The Acculturation of Internationally Educated Health Professionals in Canada", *Occupational Therapy Now*, Vol. 8, No. 3, pp. 22-25, May.

Vujicic, M. *et al.* (2004), "The Role of Wages in the Migration of Health Care Professionals from Developing Countries", *Human Resources for Health*, Vol. 2, No. 3.

Wagner S. *et al.* (2002), "A Catalogue of Current Strategies for Healthy Workplaces", Report commissioned for the Canadian Nursing Advisory Committee, Ottawa.

Wanless, D. (2002), "Securing our Future Health. Taking a Long Term View", Final Report, H.M. Treasury, London.

Watson, D.E *et al.* (2004), "Family Physician Workloads and Access to Care in Winnipeg: 1991-2001", *Canadian Medical Association Journal*, Vol. 171, No. 4, 17 August.

Weiner, J. (2005), "Prepaid Group Practice Staffing and US Physician Supply: Lessons for Workforce Policy. What Can We Learn from Examining the Staffing Levels of Some of the Country's Largest Organized Delivery Systems?", *Health Affairs*, Web Exclusive, pp. W 4.43-59.

Weiner, J.P. (2007), "Expanding the US Medical Workforce: Global Perspectives and Parallels", *British Medical Journal*, Vol. 335, pp. 236-239.

Wennberg, J.E. and M.M. Cooper (eds.) (1998), *The Dartmouth Atlas of Health Care 1998*, American Health Association Press, Chicago.

West, M.A. *et al.* (2002), "The Link between the Management of Employees and Patient Mortality in Acute Hospitals", *International Journal of Human Resource Management*, Vol. 13, No. 8, pp. 1299-1310.

WHO – World Health Organization (2006), *World Health Report 2006: Working Together for Health*, WHO, Geneva.

Wiskow, C. (2006), "Health Worker Migration Flows in Europe: Overview and Case Studies in Selected CEE Countries (Romania, the Czech Republic, Serbia and Croatia)", Working Paper No. 45, ILO, Geneva.

World Bank (2006), *Close to Home: The Development Impact of Remittances in Latin America*, Washington.

Young, R. and B. Leese (1999), "Recruitment and Retention of General Practitioners in the UK: What Are the Problems and Solutions?", *British Journal of General Practice*, Vol. 49, pp. 829-833.

Zurn, P. and J.C. Dumont (2008), "Health Workforce and International Migration: Can New Zealand Compete?", OECD Health Working Paper, No. 34, OECD, Paris.

Zurn, P., C. Dolea and B. Stilwell (2005), "Nurse Retention and Recruitment: Developing a Motivated Workforce", Issue Paper No. 4, International Council of Nurses, Geneva.

ISBN 978-92-64-05043-3
The Looming Crisis in the Health Workforce:
How Can OECD Countries Respond?
© OECD 2008

ANNEX A

Age Distribution of Physician and Nurse Workforce in Selected OECD Countries, 1995, 2000 and 2005

Australia, employed medical pratictioners by age group, 1995, 2000 and 2004

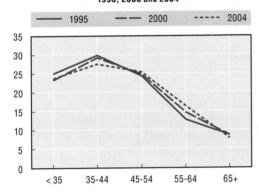

Source: Australian Institute of Health and Welfare.

Belgium, health professionals by age group, 1995, 2000 and 2005

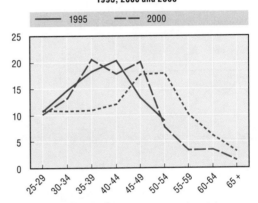

Source: European Union Labour Force Survey (data provided by Eurostat).

Canada, registered doctors by age group, 2000 and 2005

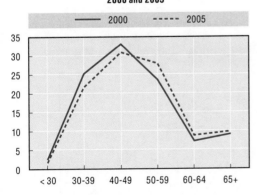

Source: Canadian Institute for Health Information.

France, active physicians by age group, 1995,1995 and 2005

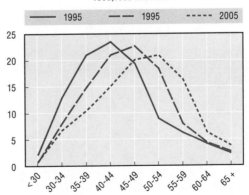

Source: Ministère de la Santé et des Solidarités, DREES.

Germany, health professionals by age group, 1995, 2000 and 2005

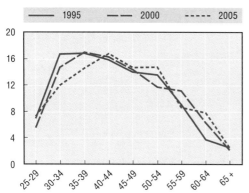

Source: European Union Labour Force Survey (data provided by Eurostat).

New Zealand, active medical workforce by age group, 1990, 1994 and 2003

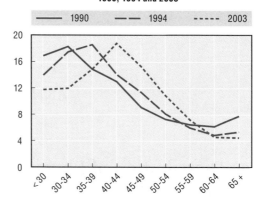

Source: NZHIS.

United Kingdom, health professionals by age group, 1995, 2000 and 2005

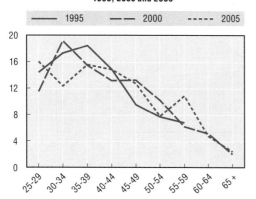

Source: European Union Labour Force Survey (data provided by Eurostat).

United States, active physicians by age group, 1985, 1995 and 2004

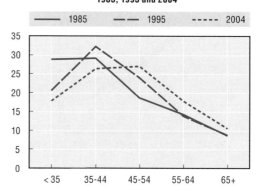

Source: American Medical Association.

Australia, employed registered nurses by age group, 1995, 2000 and 2004

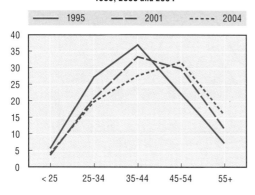

Source: Australian Institute of Health and Welfare.

England, qualified nurses midwives and health visiting staff, 1995 and 2005

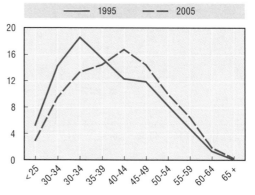

Source: NHS Information Centre.

France, employed nurses by age group, 2001 and 2005

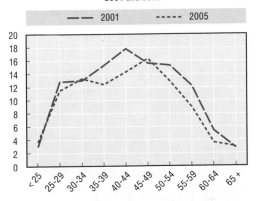

Source: Ministère de la Santé et des Solidarités, DREES.

New Zealand, registered nurses and midwives by age group, 1994, 2000 and 2004

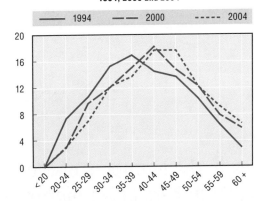

Source: NZHIS.

United States, registered nurses by age group, 1995, 2000 and 2005

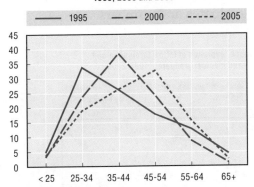

Source: National Sample Survey Registered Nurses, NSSRN and current population survey.

StatLink 🔗 http://dx.doi.org/10.1787/448366353308

ANNEX B

Changes in the Numbers of Medical and Nursing Graduates and Numbers of Immigrant Physicians and Nurses in Selected OECD Countries, 1995-2005

Figure B.1. **Changes in the numbers of medical graduates and numbers of immigrant physicians**

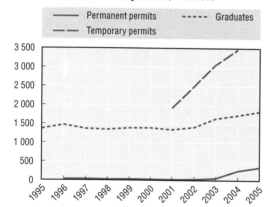

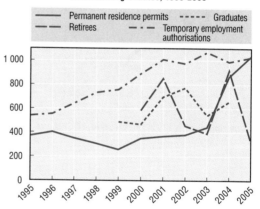

Source: Permanent residence permits: Skill Stream – Principal Applicants Only; Work Permits: visa subclass 422 and 457; *OECD Health Data 2007.*

Source: Citizenship and Immigration Canada, Facts & Figures 2005. Permanent residence permits: Permanent Residents in (Intended) Health Care Occupations (Principal Applicants); Temporary employment authorisations: Annual Flow of Foreign Workers and *OECD Health Data 2007.*

Figure B.1. **Changes in the numbers of medical graduates and numbers of immigrant physicians** (*cont.*)

Source: The authorization registry of the National Board of Health and *OECD Health Data 2007*.

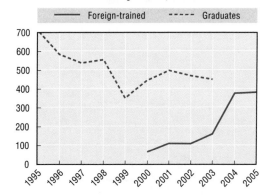

Source: National Authority for Medicolegal Affairs and *OECD Health Data 2007*.

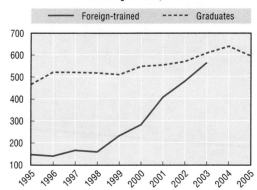

Source: Full Registration Medical Council and *OECD Health Data 2007*.

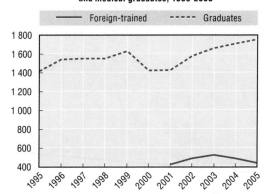

Source: Big register and *OECD Health Data 2007*.

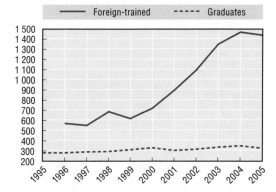

Source: Medical Council New Zealand and *OECD Health Data 2007*.

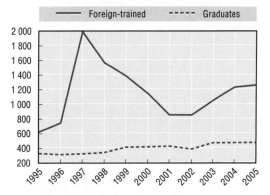

Source: Statens autorisasjonskontor for helsepersonell and *OECD Health Data 2007*.

Figure B.1. **Changes in the numbers of medical graduates and numbers of immigrant physicians** (cont.)

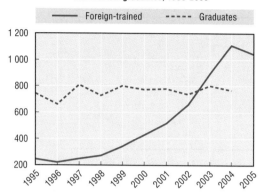

Sweden, evolution of inflow foreign-trained and medical graduates, 1995-2005

Source: National Board of Health and Welfare and *OECD Health Data 2007.*

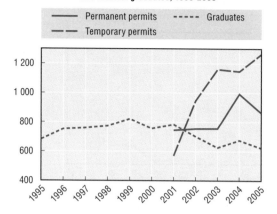

Switzerland, evolution of inflow foreign-trained and medical graduates, 1995-2005

Source: Office fédéral des migrations ODM and *OECD Health Data 2007.*

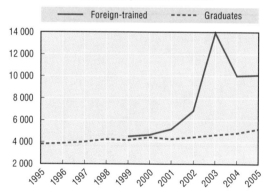

United Kingdom, evolution of inflow foreign-trained and medical graduates, 1995-2005

Source: General Medical Council – new full registrations and *OECD Health Data 2007.*

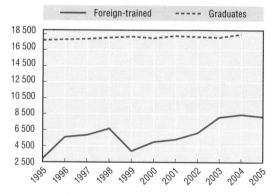

United States, evolution of inflow foreign-trained and medical graduates, 1995-2005

Source: MD Physicians completing USMLE step 3 and *OECD Health Data 2007.*

StatLink ᴍᴤᴸ http://dx.doi.org/10.1787/448420165461

Figure B.2. **Changes in the numbers of nursing graduates and numbers of immigrant nurses**

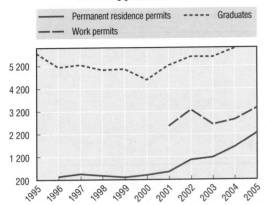

Australia, evolution of inflow foreign-trained and nursing graduates, 1995-2005

Source: Permanent residence permits: Skill Stream – Principal Applicants Only; Work Permits: visa subclass 422 and 457; *OECD Health Data 2007.*

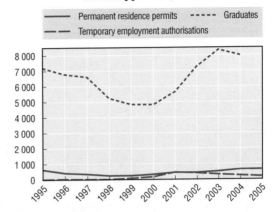

Canada, evolution of inflow foreign-trained and nursing graduates, 1995-2005

Source: Citizenship and Immigration Canada, Facts & Figures 2005. Permanent residence permits: Permanent Residents in (Intended) Health Care Occupations (Principal Applicants); Temporary employment authorisations: Annual Flow of Foreign Workers and *OECD Health Data 2007.*

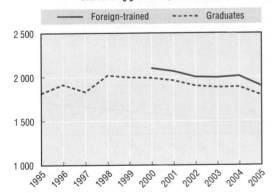

Denmark, evolution of inflow foreign-trained and nursing graduates, 1995-2005

Source: The authorization registry of the National Board of Health and *OECD Health Data 2007.*

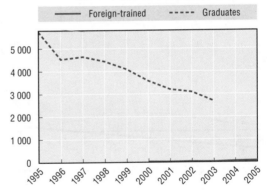

Finland, evolution of inflow foreign-trained and nursing graduates, 1995-2005

Source: National Authority for Medicolegal Affairs and OECD *Health Data 2007.*

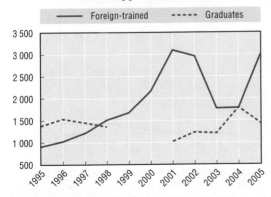

Ireland, evolution of inflow foreign-trained and nursing graduates, 1995-2005

Source: An bord altranais and *OECD Health Data 2007.*

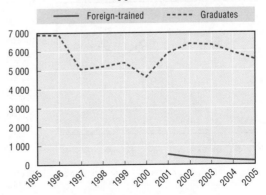

Netherlands, evolution of inflow foreign-trained and nursing graduates, 1995-2005

Source: Big register and *OECD Health Data 2007.*

Figure B.2. **Changes in the numbers of nursing graduates and numbers of immigrant nurses** (cont.)

New Zealand, evolution of inflow foreign-trained and nursing graduates, 1995-2005

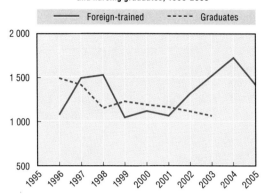

Source: Nursing Council New Zealand and *OECD Health Data 2007.*

Norway, evolution of inflow foreign-trained and nursing graduates, 1995-2005

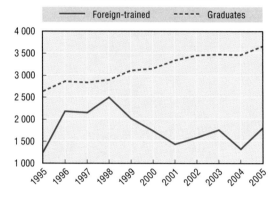

Source: Statens autorisasjonskontor for helsepersonell and *OECD Health Data 2007.*

Sweden, evolution of inflow foreign-trained and nursing graduates, 1995-2005

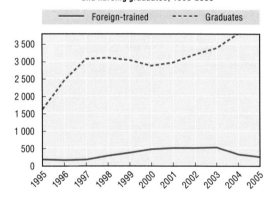

Source: National Board of Health and Welfare and *OECD Health Data 2007.*

Switzerland, evolution of inflow foreign-trained and nursing graduates, 1995-2005

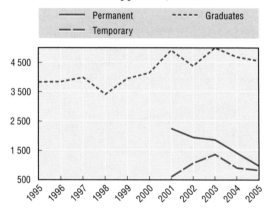

Source: Office fédéral des migrations ODM and *OECD Health Data 2007.*

United Kingdom, evolution of inflow foreign-trained and nursing graduates, 1995-2005

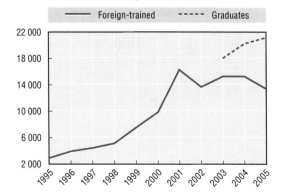

Source: Nursing and Midwifery Council – new registrations and *OECD Health Data 2007.*

United States, evolution of inflow foreign-trained and nursing graduates, 1995-2005

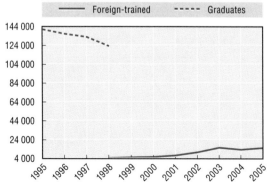

Source: National council of state boards of nursing passed NCLEX-RN exams and *OECD Health Data 2007.*

StatLink 🔗 *http://dx.doi.org/10.1787/448433803717*

ANNEX C

Medical and Nursing Education Systems in Selected OECD Countries

Country	DOCTORS — Numerical limits apply to medical education	DOCTORS — Remarks	DOCTORS — Recent change in intakes	NURSES — Numerical limits apply to nursing education	NURSES — Remarks	NURSES — Recent change in intakes
Australia	Yes	Controlled by the Commonwealth through funding university places	Five new medical schools have opened since 2000 and seven more programmes are planned for 2008	Yes	Places in nursing schools, for registered nurse education, are determined by universities but the Commonwealth provides some funding and sets a minimum number of places for basic nurse education	The Higher Education Support Act of 2003 provided a significant increase in the number of nursing places
Austria	No	Since 2003 Austria has one private medical school		Yes	Federal states determine the number of places available in nursing schools	
Belgium	Yes since 1997	Government fixes the number of new accreditation to practice	Decreased to 600 in 2006 (60% Flemish-speaking and 40% French-speaking students)	No		
Canada	Yes	Medical education is essentially a provincial responsibility		No	Provincial/territorial governments provide funding to post-secondary educational institutions. Places in nursing schools are based on negotiation between the ministries of health and education	
France	Yes since 1971	A decree from the Prime Minister fixes the numerus clausus for the admission in the second year of undergraduate medical school	Increased progressively since 1993 to 7 100 in 2007, with the objective to reach 8 000 by 2012	Yes	Quota for students at national level	The cap went from 1981 in 1997-98 to 30 000 in 2003-04
Germany	Yes	Study places are allocated by the Central Office for the Allocation of Places in Higher Education according to a procedure established by the Federal Lander.		No	Places available in nursing schools are determined by the Federal Länder	
Greece	Yes	The Ministry of Education determines the number of places in each medical school on the basis of available financial resources rather than to match demand and supply	The number of new students entering medical school has been recently stabilised	Yes	The Ministry of Education and the Central Health Council determine the places in public nursing schools	
Ireland	No	There are a certain number of state-funded places, but colleges have discretion to take in more students		Yes	Places available in nursing schools are determined by the Higher Education Authority and funded by the Department of Health and Children	
Italy	Yes	The number of places for the degree in Medicine and Surgery is determined yearly by a decree of the Minister for Universities and Research	In 2007, the number of places was fixed at 7 858	Yes		
Japan	Yes		The medical school intake is limited until 2020 (around 7 000)	Yes	Places available in nursing schools are determined jointly by national and prefecture governments	

	DOCTORS			NURSES		
	Numerical limits apply to medical education	Remarks	Recent change in intakes	Numerical limits apply to nursing education	Remarks	Recent change in intakes
Korea	Yes		Six new medical schools were opened in the 1990s but the medical school intake was cut by 10% in 2007	Yes	Places available in nursing schools are determined by the government.	
Mexico	Yes		The number of medical schools increased from 27 in 1970 to 56 in 1979. Between 1970 and 1980, student enrolment more than tripled but it has decreased since	No		
Netherlands	Yes		On average 2 500 students are admitted each year	No		
New Zealand	Yes	Enrolment into medical school is capped financially	The cap has been set at 325 since 2004. It has been lifted twice in the last 20 years	No		
Norway	Yes			No		
Spain	Yes	The Ministries of Health and Education and the National Conference of University Chairmen set the cap		Yes	The number of places available in nursing schools is determined by the Ministries of Health and Education	The number of nursing places was limited in the late 1990s to about 7 000
Sweden	Yes	Medical school intake is controlled by the central government		Yes	The number of places available in nursing schools is determined by the government	
Switzerland	Yes since 1998	Some cantons have introduced a *numerus clauses*		Yes	The number of places available in nursing schools is determined by cantons	
United Kingdom	Yes	Medical school intake is controlled by the government through the funding of university places	Medical school intake nearly doubled, from 3 200 in 1990 to more than 6 000 in 2005-06.	Yes	Places available in nursing schools are determined in partnership between the Department of Health and local Workforce Development Confederations. Higher education institutions may provide additional places for students who fund their own courses	
United States	Yes	The US federal government does not impose any limitation on medical school enrolment, but residency places (funded by Medicare) are capped. States contribute to finance undergraduate training (through Medicaid)	Places in allopathic schools were frozen at their 1980 levels for more than two decades. In the mid-1990, few new osteopathic colleges were established (more in the recent years)	No	There is no central authority that determines the number of places available in nursing schools, although the states' decisions on public nursing education funding has a direct impact on capacity	

Source: Adapted from Simoens and Hurst (2006), Simoens et al. (2005) and Hall et al. (2003).

OECD PUBLICATIONS, 2, rue André-Pascal, 75775 PARIS CEDEX 16
PRINTED IN FRANCE
(81 2008 14 1 P) ISBN 978-92-64-05043-3 – No. 56371 2008